A Guide to

The National Museum of Ireland

A Guide to
The National Museum
of Ireland

Patrick F. Wallace

Photography Valerie Dowling

TOWN
HOUSE
DUBLIN

In association with The National Museum of Ireland

First published in 2000 by

Town House and Country House
Trinity House, Charleston Rd
Ranelagh, Dublin 6

In association with
The National Museum of Ireland
Kildare Street,
Dublin 2.

PBK ISBN: 1-86059-057-8
HBK ISBN: 1-86059-056-X

Typeset by Typeform Repro Ltd.

Printed in Italy by MILANOSTAMPA

Dr Patrick Wallace has been Director of the National Museum of Ireland since 1988. Before that he was the archaeologist in charge of the museum's excavations at Wood Quay. He is well known for his work on the Viking Age, especially the archaeology of Dublin itself, and also for popularising the museum and archaeology on radio and television, not least through his series Legacy/Oidhreacht which was broadcast in English and Irish versions.

Contents

Acknowledgements

In thanking my colleagues for their help with information and in some cases for their publications, which I have anthologised, may I single out Mairéad Dunlevy, Eamonn Kelly, Mary Cahill, Raghnall O'Floinn, Michael Kenny, Clare McCutcheon, Lorraine McClean, Michael Heffernan and Sharon Fogarty for special thanks. My greatest debt is to our senior museum photographer, Valerie Dowling, whose work I have allowed to influence many of my choices. I sincerely trust that any glory reflected by the objects illustrated here will redound to the credit not only of the present generation of curators and conservators – and indeed the services, conservation and administrative staffs – but mainly of our predecessors for their education, enlightenment, patriotism and commitment to a future that resulted in our having responsibility for the care and protection of such marvellous and varied collections, collections that define Ireland itself and make our institution Ireland's great interpretative centre.

Grateful acknowledgement is made to the Institute of Certified Public Accountants in Ireland for their sponsorship towards the cost of producing this guidebook.

Introduction

This guidebook is intended primarily as a souvenir – something for visitors to the National Museum of Ireland to take away with them – rather than as a book to use during the course of a visit. Such a record can offer but a flavour of what the museum contains, a selection of artefacts made on behalf of the visitor by the director of the museum. Regrettably, given its scope as a memento of the museum, this book can be neither a history of an institution that has developed its collection over almost three centuries, nor a description of the three main Dublin venues that now house the museum's collections: Kildare Street (Archaeology), Merrion Street (Natural History) and Collins Barracks (Decorative Arts and History).

My choice of objects in the present selection has been determined not so much by the bias of my own area of interest and expertise, which is the archaeology of the early Middle Ages and Viking Dublin as well as social history; rather, I have chosen some of the great prehistoric and early Christian treasures of Ireland, with which the museum's name is synonymous and which visitors expect to see when they come to the museum. I have included also with these great treasures a selection of items from the applied arts and history collections, some of which are now on show at Collins Barracks, as well as a few items from the folklife collections, which are destined for display at our branch at Castlebar. And, for the sake of completeness, I have also made a small selection from natural history which is on display in the Natural History Museum, Merrion Street.

The Natural History Museum dates from the 1850s and our Kildare Street premises from 1888. Collins Barracks is an eighteenth-century complex, though it was opened as a museum only in 1997. The Barracks has witnessed almost three centuries of Irish history, not least the death of Wolfe Tone as well as some of his supporters in 1798. These are now, appropriately, commemorated in the Croppies' Acre at the riverward side of our main museum presence at the Barracks. It is planned that Collins Barracks will, over the next few years, be developed to become our main exhibition centre, as well as our administrative headquarters.

The groups of collections that make up our National Museum constitute what in European terms is styled a 'comprehensive museum'. The range of collections varies from archaeology to natural history (including geology), to folklore, history and the decorative arts. These collections are far too eclectic and, in some ways, unconnected (other than that together they constitute the physical record of portable heritage of Ireland, as well as its settings) to be fairly treated in any introductory book, especially one purporting to be the personal selection of somebody who comes with the background bias of one of the four main curatorial areas.

Nevertheless, I hope the visitor will gain something of the quality of the preservation of the artefacts and the burial remains from our Stone and Bronze Ages (on display in the Prehistoric exhibition at Kildare Street), the magnificence of some of our unparalleled Bronze Age gold exhibition Ór (also on display in the Centre Court), the sophistication of the art and design of the late Celtic metalworkers and the variety of the artefacts and techniques they employed in what was Ireland's greatest age of all, the golden age of early Christianity (roughly ad 600–800), when such treasures as the Ardagh Chalice, the Tara Brooch and the Derrynaflan Paten were produced on this island. This last group is on display in the museum's Treasury, where it is complemented by an audio-visual show.

The absorption of the various influences of the Vikings – be they urban, commercial, numismatic, technological or artistic – by the Irish should be evident from the upstairs galleries and the related audio-visual theatre devoted to them. The visitor will find our Viking Ireland exhibition, which contains items from the Wood Quay excavations, upstairs alongside our medieval Ireland exhibition, on the balcony off which, incidentally, you will find our Ancient Egypt display.

Although the excitement of our modernised approach to exhibitions at Collins Barracks cannot come across in the small selection of applied arts examples which have to represent entire new galleries devoted to subjects such as silver and furniture, I hope my selection signals the existence of these great collections. While also rare in the present selection, the potential of the folklife collection – which is so complementary to art and industry and indeed necessary for the explanation of the historical and archaeological collections – should also come through, as should the potential for future displays of our exotic ethnographical collections. I hope the visitor to Collins Barracks will be able to savour the silver and furniture galleries as well as the costume and jewellery display.

These are great times in the on-going story of our institution. We have got the storage and exhibition spaces, as well as the conservation laboratory, our predecessors craved for so long. With the opening of the Folklife Museum at Castlebar, and the building of the second phase at Collins Barracks, where our geological and ethnographical collections as well as history and militaria will go on display, we will finally be seen to be doing justice to the great collections which have been entrusted to our care. The realisation of a gallery of the twentieth century, in which design history will feature, is a cherished personal ambition which I also hope to realise. Nobody realises better than the museum worker the transient nature of life, work and responsibility. I trust the watch of our generation will be perceived as fruitful by our successors. The award of staff numbers commensurate with the responsibilities and the potential of the collections could make this a great period. The implementation of the new Cultural Institutions Act will signal its arrival. If, by illustrating a tiny section of our collections, this souvenir highlights their uniqueness and draws attention to them, the writer will be well served.

Patrick F. Wallace
Director

March 2000

1 Neolithic pots from Annagh CO. LIMERICK

One of the most compact groups of burial monuments from the Irish Neolithic period (about 4000–2000 BC) is the dozen or so burials in which a large sub-megalithic cist is placed in the centre of a kerbed mound or cairn. Many such cists have produced evidence for two or more human remains, the skeletons being mostly unburnt and articulated. The burials are usually accompanied by a limited range of grave goods, particularly decorated pots. Recent radiocarbon dating places these burials near the beginning of the Neolithic, a date also confirmed for a related series of burials found within or behind natural caves and/or large boulders. The pots from Annagh were found with four unburnt skeletons (two flexed and one disturbed) along with a perforated antler, as well as a flint knife, arrowhead and blade. The bones have been carbon-dated to between 3600 and 3400 BC.

H:8.5cm, W: 17.6cm; H: 8.8cm, W: 15cm   NMI REG. NOS 92: E47: 5/6

2 Stone object from Knowth, CO. MEATH

The great burial mound at Knowth contains two passage tombs. The stone object featured here was found outside the entrance to the western tomb in 1970. The phallic object is likely to have been used in a fertility ceremony. The stone is decorated with a broad band of horizontal U-shaped grooves, interrupted by a tapering vertical groove. It dates to about 3000–2500 BC.

L: 25.5cm, W at base: 3.8cm

3 Knowth macehead, CO. MEATH

This ceremonial macehead of polished flint from the passage tomb at Knowth is one of the most imposing prestige objects to have survived from the Irish Neolithic period. It dates to about 2500 BC and was found lying on the old ground surface between the jamb stones at the entrance to the eastern tomb's right-hand recess. The quality of the decoration on such a hard material is unparalleled in Ireland. The relative positioning of the hole, the spirals and the fluting on one of the ends suggest that this object was possibly meant to resemble a human head.

W: 8.2cm, H: 54cm

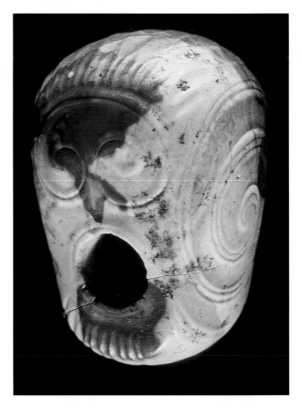

4 Tedavnet gold discs,
CO. MONAGHAN

'Sun-discs' were possibly the earliest metal objects produced in Ireland. They are often found in pairs and have centrally located perforations, which suggest that they were attached to clothes and worn as jewellery. They date to the time of the first metalworking in Ireland, to the beginning of our Early Bronze Age, about 2000 BC. The discs are made from sheet gold, with the decoration produced by a combination of repoussé (pushed out from the back) and punching techniques.

D: 11.3; 11.5cm
NMI REG. NO. 1872.34/35

5 Carrowkeel beads and pendants
CO. SLIGO

The stone beads and pendants shown here are typical of those found in Irish passage tombs. This set was recovered from the Carrowkeel cemetery.

NMI REG. NO: E624:21–52

6 Early Bronze Age funerary pottery

Pottery vessels are by far the most common burial accompaniment of the Early Bronze Age, about 2000–1200 BC. The surviving vessels are of three types: those that were made to contain offerings, known by archaeologists as 'food vessels'; a larger 'urn' type vessel; and a tiny 'pygmy cup' series. All were made by building up coils of clay, which were then fired at low temperatures.

'Food vessels', which are thought to have derived from the preceding Beaker tradition, have been categorised as belonging to either 'bowl' or 'vase' traditions. Those of the 'bowl' tradition are usually from 10cm to 15cm high and are often highly decorated with rectilinear motifs and (on the bases) cross shapes. 'Bowls' are usually found with cremated or unburnt bones in stone, box-like cist graves and, less commonly, in pits. 'Vases', which usually accompany cremations, are occasionally large and contain burnt remains. Other urn traditions used either cordoned or collared vessels, the former named after their decoration of horizontal cordons and the latter after the distinctive neck.

7 Bronze Age metalwork

The Irish Bronze Age witnessed the introduction of a series of revolutionary improvements to the bronzesmith's craft. Indeed, the first use of copper in the couple of centuries before 2000 BC was most significant; weapons and tools could now be shaped in moulds, edges could be sharpened and old bronzes melted down for re-use.

The introduction of better moulds, such as those of clay, in the Later Bronze Age meant that the means of attaching that central artefact of the Bronze Age, the axe or hatchet, to its handle were constantly improving. The palstave followed the axe and finally the socketed axe allowed the implement actually to grip its own handle. The production of more agricultural implements such as sickles became possible, as did a variety of spearheads and the popular leaf-shaped sword. This was to be the main weapon of a new warrior/aristocratic class. The use of swords led in turn to improvements in shield production. Sheet bronzeworking was also used in the production of complicated buckets and cauldrons.

8 Derrinboy armlets CO. OFFALY

Made of thick sheet gold, these bracelets were found during turf-cutting in 1959 along with two gold tress rings and a coiled gold wire necklet. The hoard has been dated to the beginning of the Later Bronze Age, 1200–1000 BC. The decoration on the armlets consists of six raised bands of punched ridges, alternating with plain raised bands, all laid out parallel to the length of the gold strips before they were folded into cylinders. These distinctive Irish bracelets are now regarded as being of southern British inspiration, with possibly some continental influence in the background.

H: 7.1; 7.2cm   NMI REG. NOS. 1959.693/694

9 Bishopsland hoard CO. KILDARE

This hoard of a bronzesmith's/carpenter's tools gives its name to the earliest phase of Ireland's Later Bronze Age, 1200–1000 BC. It was found in 1942 some 46cm below the surface of a slope leading to a river. The deposition of such hoards commenced as urn burial ceased, suggesting that they may have been part of some newly introduced burial ritual whereby personal objects were deposited in the earth instead of in a grave. It is likely that the tools were the property of a versatile craftsman. They include a palstave, a socketed axehead, a flat chisel and a trunnion chisel, all of which were used for felling or working wood; hammerheads, a graver, an anvil, a vice, a piece of solid bronze, wire and a rod, which suggest a metalworker; a sickle belonging to a farmer; a saw and a series of more personal possessions including finger-rings, a bracelet, tweezers, toilet article, flesh-hook and a tube of unknown function. All in all, the varied possessions of a significant person in Later Bronze Age society.

NMI REG. NOS. 1942.1756–1772; 1944.148–149

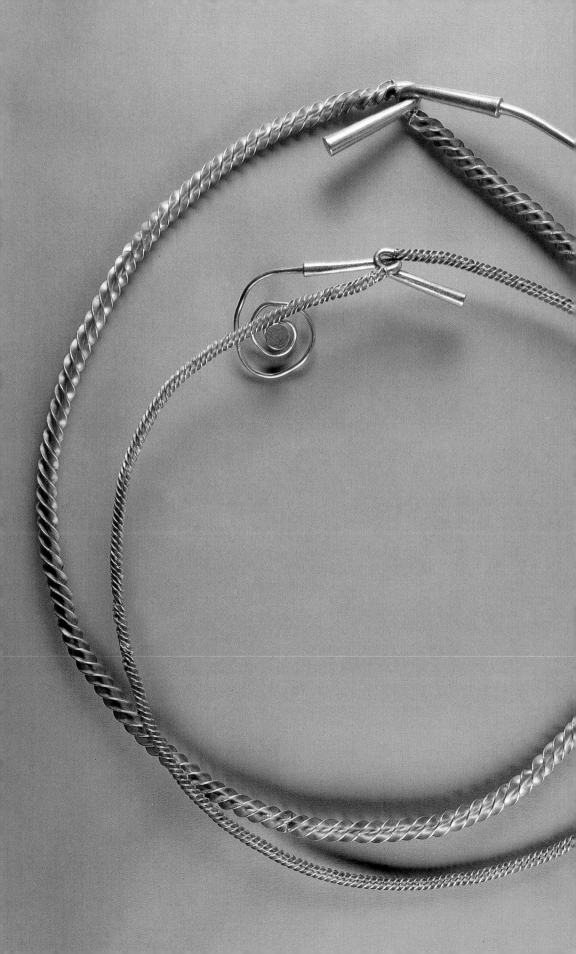

10 Gold Torcs from Tara CO. MEATH

Torcs are twisted lengths or strips of gold or bronze, *torquere* being the Latin word for 'twist'. The production of twisted gold ornaments began in Ireland about 1200 BC, when local goldsmiths appear to have come under the influence of British and continental craftworkers, who themselves received many new ideas, technical and otherwise, from the east Mediterranean/Near East area.

Both of the torcs shown here are of the four-flanged type, i.e. those that were hammered up from square or rectangular-sectioned bars of gold before being twisted very tightly. It is thought that the elaborate terminals were soldered on to the torcs, then turned back to lock into one another. The extent of their respective diameters suggests that they could have been worn around the waist. The two torcs were found together about 1810 near the Rath of the Synods at Tara.

L: 37cm; 43cm   NMI REG NOS. W.173; W172

11 Gold earrings, Castlerea CO. ROSCOMMON

This pair of flange-twisted gold earrings dates from the beginning of the Later Bronze Age, about 1200 BC. They belong to the 'torc' group of ornaments, which includes twisted gold and bronze items made for wearing on the arms, wrists, neck and possibly the ankles and waist. This pair was made by hammering out the edges of a rectangular-sectioned gold bar which was then twisted. A biconical bead-like terminal and a spike were added at either end. It is uncertain whether such earrings were influenced by the Mediterranean tradition of soldering two angled strips of gold together before twisting, or whether the technique evolved in Britain and Ireland.

W: 3.4cm; 3.5cm   NMI REG. NOS. W63; W64

12 Ballytegan hoard CO. LAOIS

This Late Bronze Age hoard, found in a sandpit in 1967, dates to the seventh/eighth century BC. It is valuable for the variety of disc-headed pins and ring types it contains and for their association with one another. It is also of interest for the association of gold-foil-covered ornaments with bronzes, and for the varied treatment of the decoration on the delicately applied gold foil. Shown here, from left to right, are a three-strand bronze 'torc ring', a bronze disc-headed pin with the disc at right angles to the stem, a pair of bronze disc-headed or 'sunflower' pins with applied gold foil on their front faces, a large bronze disc-headed or 'sunflower' pin, a pair of cast bronze socketed axeheads, a pair of large bronze rings, ten smaller bronze rings, a solid double ring, a solid ring with a pair of smaller rings attached, a cast bronze cylindrical ingot and a cylinder of thirty-four bronze wire rings. The two gold-covered pins are among the delights of Late Bronze Age metalwork, mainly because of their restraint and sophistication, which is somewhat at variance with the greater exuberance of most contemporary goldwork.

L: 19.2cm, D: 5.9cm; L: 19.8cm, D: 6cm   NMI REG NOS. 1967:2,3

13 Mooghaun collar CO. CLARE

Made of heavy sheet gold, this collar is one of six found during the construction of the Limerick–Ennis railway in 1854, when the largest hoard of gold objects ever uncovered in Europe turned up in swampy ground not far from the large stone fort at Mooghaun. The hoard is dated to the seventh/eighth century BC, and the fort itself is even earlier (about 1000 BC). Although the bulk of the hoard was melted down, casts and drawings were made which convey some idea of the size, weight and overall magnificence of what is rightly termed the 'great Clare gold hoard'.

While the Mooghaun collars are unique, it is thought that they show some influence from the northern European Late Bronze Age. It has also been suggested that along with the torcs of the earlier phase of the Later Bronze Age (see No. 10), the Mooghaun collars played a part in the genesis of the great gold collars of Gleninsheen type (see No. 17).

W: 161cm   NMI REG. NO. W26

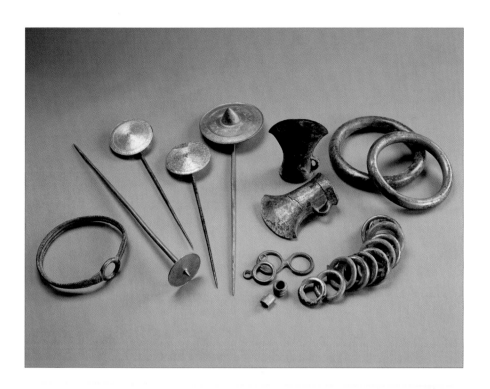

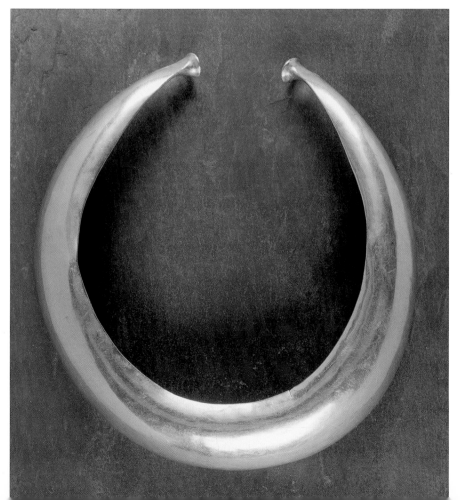

14 Lough Gur shield
CO. LIMERICK

This sheet bronze shield dates to the seventh/eighth century BC. It was found in a bog near Lough Gur, the site of so many discoveries from the Stone, Bronze and Iron Ages. It is the finest and largest example of bronze sheet metalwork from the Late Bronze Age in Ireland. It is also one of the most vivid examples of that war-like phase of our prehistory. This particular item was probably used for parade purposes and would have offered little resistance to the contemporary bronze sword. Smaller beaten bronze shields as well as wooden and leather shields (which may also be seen in the National Museum) were much better equipped to survive the hand-to-hand combat of the time.

D: 71.3cm   NMI Reg. No. 1872.15

15 Castlederg cauldron
CO. TYRONE

This seventh-century BC riveted sheet bronze cauldron is a prime example of the Irish Late Bronze Age metalworker's skill in sheet bronze. The ability to attain the highest standards in casting bronze is also evident from the cast ring-handles and their retaining staples, for which clay moulds and the lost wax technique would have had to be deployed. This cauldron type is based on Greek prototypes, with the conical-headed rivet derived from central Europe. Presumably such cauldrons were filled with water and used as cooking pots, suspended by their rings over fires. It has been suggested that the heads of the rivets both retained and distributed the heat.

Max D: 56cm, D at rim: 46cm, internal D: 40.2cm, D of handles: 12.2cm   NMI REG NO. 1933.119

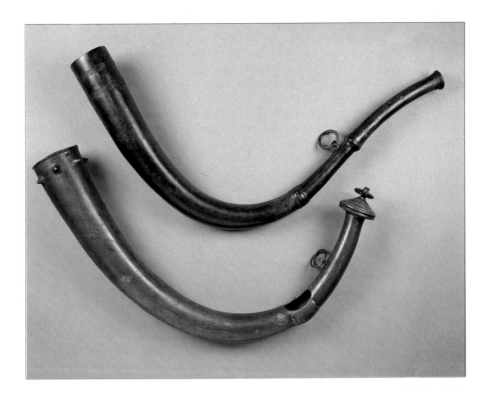

16 Cast bronze horns from Drumbest and Drunkendult CO. ANTRIM

Over half of the Bronze Age horns of Europe and the Middle East have been found in Ireland. There were two types of cast bronze horn in seventh-century BC Ireland, one blown from the side and the other from the end. The body of the Drumbest specimen was cast as two separate pieces in clay moulds; these were joined together later. It was found in a bog in Co. Antrim along with three other specimens. The Drunkendult horn was also made in a clay mould, but the mould elements were poorly lined up (as the seam shows). It also came from a bog in Co. Antrim and was found with part of another horn.

These horns are significant for the information they have shed not only on Bronze Age music, but also on the technical prowess of the bronzesmiths. It is thought that the end-blow horns were played like the Australian didgeridoo, giving a good harmonic and rhythmic base. The end-blows occur mainly in the south-west of Ireland. The side-blows are not found outside of Ireland.

Drumbest L: 89.5cm, D at mouth: 7cm   NMI REG. NO. 1893.17   Drunkendult L: 58.5cm, D at mouth: 6.5cm
NMI REG. NO. 1930.107

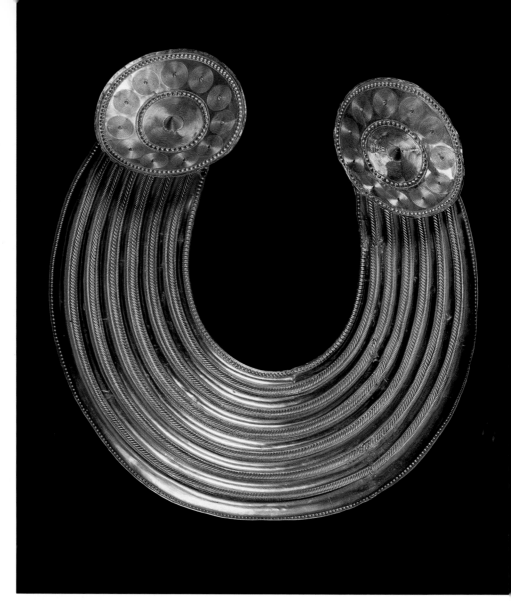

17 Gleninsheen collar or gorget CO. CLARE

About eight collars of this sheet-gold type are known from the Irish Later Bronze Age. They are the most spectacular of the sheet-gold ornaments produced about the seventh century BC, the most magnificent being the Gleninsheen specimen, which was found concealed in a rock fissure in the Burren, Co. Clare, in 1932. All the collars were found in the area around the mouth of the Shannon and all but one are in the National Museum.

Each of the collars consists of a wide U-shaped sheet of gold, onto which a pair of double-plated discs was sewn to cover a plain, straight-cut end. The Gleninsheen specimen has several parallel plain ridges pushed up from the back. Between these, a large rope-patterned line is flanked on either side by smaller lines of rope pattern. The inner and outer edges display single lines of domes. The decoration on the faces of the terminals consists of a pointed boss surrounded by concentric circles, and midway by a series of dots, beyond which is a wide band of eleven cone and circle motifs.

Max lateral W of collar: 31.4cm, max W of collar: 10.5cm, D. of terminals: 10–10.2cm   NMI REG. NO. 1934.85

18 Gold boxes from Ballinclemesig
CO. KERRY and Mullingar
CO. WESTMEATH

These sheet-gold boxes, which date to about the eighth century BC, are often regarded as containers, yet the discovery of a gold ball in one found recently at Ballinesker, Co. Wexford, would suggest that they may have been used as ceremonial rattles. The arrangement of the design and the use of the concentric circle motif parallels the ornament on the terminal discs of the contemporary collars or gorgets (see No. 17), while the concentric ladder pattern in the Mullingar box parallels the ornament on the gold-foil-covered disc-headed pins from Ballytegan, Co. Laois (see No. 12).

Ballinclemesig D: 6.4cm   NMI REG. NO. 1975.256;
Mullingar D: 5.6cm   NMI REG. NO. 1884.8/9

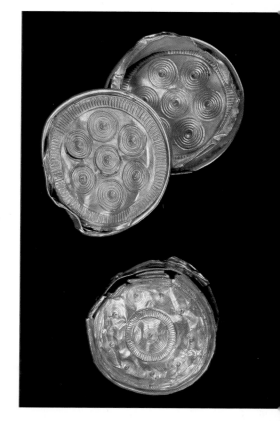

19 Gold-foil-covered 'bulla'
CO. KILDARE

Irish goldsmiths produced a variety of ornaments in the seventh and eighth centuries bc. The 'bulla' illustrated here, which was given its name from the Latin word for a pouch, is the most celebrated of its type, not simply because of the skill that was involved in covering lead with thin gold foil, or because of the variety and symmetry with which the geometric design is arranged on the front, back and top surfaces, but also because the arrangement of the U-shaped motifs is thought by some to give the impression of a human face on one of the surfaces. If it is, it is probably the closest we will ever get to Late Bronze Age man's attempt to represent himself.

L: 6.4cm   NMI REG. NO. W265

20 Loughnashade trumpet (detail) CO. ARMAGH

This is the finest surviving sheet-bronze trumpet of the Celtic Iron Age, and one of four placed in Loughnashade ('Lake of the Jewels') as part of a sacrificial deposit in the first century BC. The lake lies alongside the Iron Age enclosure complex known as Emain Macha or Navan Fort. The decoration on the flange at the mouth (shown here) is executed in repoussé. The ornament is abstract, a stylisation based on the classical lotus-bud motif, and is arranged in mirror-image quadrants that feature sinuous tendrils terminating in high-relief spiral bosses.

A similar large curved trumpet was depicted on the celebrated third-century BC Pergamon statue of the Dying Gaul, who, incidentally, is also shown wearing a collar of Broighter, Co. Derry, type (see No. 22).

L of convex edge: 186.5cm, L of flange: 19.3cm   NMI REG. NO. W8

21 & 22 Broighter boat and Broighter collar CO. DERRY

This little gold boat and spectacular gold collar were found along with a bowl with suspension rings, two chains and two twisted collars, all of gold, during ploughing at the end of the nineteenth century.

Probably a votive offering, the boat is the earliest representation of the contemporary ocean-going hide-covered currach. Note the mast and the steering oar. The Broighter collar, from the first century BC, is one of the most significant ornaments of the European Iron Age. The ornamentation consists of a symmetrically arranged, highly stylised interpretation of a foliage design executed in high relief. The classical lotus-bud motif was the inspiration for the main motif. Note also the openwork strip of three rows of conjoined repoussé bosses set into a recessed channel around the side of the left terminal, which gives the effect of granulation.

Boat L: 18.3cm, W: 7.51cm; collar D: 19.4cm, D of terminal: 4.45cm   NMI REG. NO. 1903.232

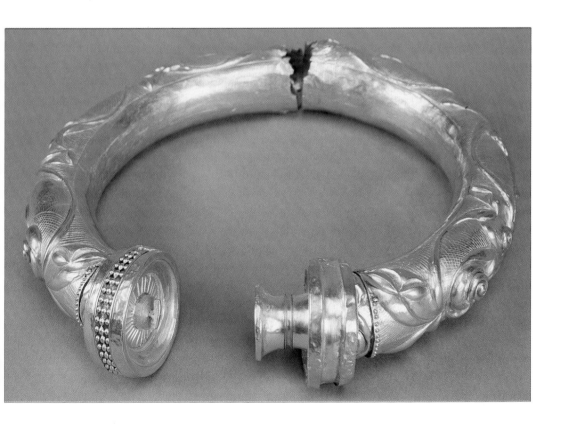

23 Keshcarrigan bowl CO. LEITRIM

This bowl, possibly a drinking cup, is thought to be of the early first century AD and was found in water between Lough Scur and Lough Marrive in Co. Leitrim. The bowl is of beaten bronze, which was probably roughly beaten into shape and smoothed while being spun into a mould, since there is what looks like a chuck-mark on the base. It is plain except for a hammered zig-zag line along the out-turned rim. The art of the object lies in the sophistication of its smooth plain lines and in the sinuous soldered-on cast bronze handle, which is in the form of a duck's head with thin neck, eye-sockets (presumably for red enamel insets) and an upturned bill that touches the rim. This stylisation or suggestion rather than an exact portrayal of an animal not only prefigures modern art by reducing form to its essential lines and confers movement on that form, but also embodies the antipathy of native artistic taste and style to representation; the inclination to stylisation, abstraction and pattern are all evident in this specimen, which was possibly imported from southern Britain.

Max D: 15.3cm, depth: 7.2cm   NMI REG. NO. W37

24 Bronze bowl from Lakill and Moortown (Fore) CO. WESTMEATH

This recently acquired bronze bowl contained a cremation burial and was found in a hill-fort at Fore. Only one of its two original handles survives. Like the roughly contemporary bowl from Keshcarrigan (see No. 23), the handle is in the shape of a bird, although in the present case this is smaller and less elegant. The middle of the bowl, which is decorated by a line of large, flat, domed studs, is of sheet bronze. It is thought to be similar to a bowl from a Celtic burial at Spettisbury Rings, Dorset, and is even more likely than the Keshcarrigan bowl to be an import from southern Britain. It dates from around the time of Christ.

H: 16.8cm, D: 28.3cm   NMI REG. NO. 1988.172

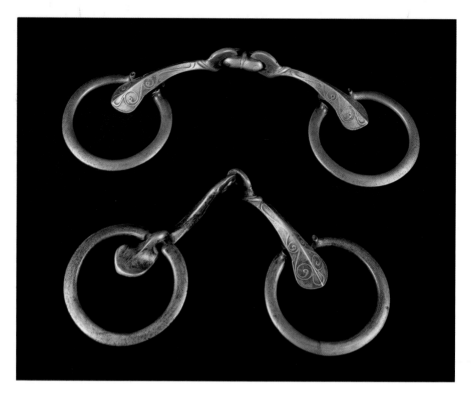

25 Attymon horse bits CO. GALWAY

These cast bronze bridle or snaffle bits are among the loveliest and most revealing of all the artefacts from the later part of the Celtic Iron Age (about the third century AD) in Ireland. Indeed, they are also among the most revealing in terms of what they tell us about the people who made and used them. They were found in a bog along with a pair of bronze Y-shaped pieces. The bits are distinctively Irish in type, and the Y-shaped pieces, which were possibly used for leading horses, are found only in Ireland. Because the bits occur in pairs, it is thought that they were used to harness horses in paired draught, possibly chariots. A yoke mount from such an arrangement was recovered from Lough Gur, Co. Limerick. The Attymon bits are well worn. The side links have raised S-scrolls or palmetted (palm-leaf type) designs on the two-faced upper surfaces. The rings are flat with stop studs and the Y-shaped pieces have exquisite raised triskeles (sets of three radiating curves) on the large semicircular knobs that occur on the shanks.

Top L: 31.8cm, max W: 8.35cm; Lower central link missing, max W: 8.55cm   NMI REG. NO. 1891.9/9a

26 Cornalaragh box lid
CO. MONAGHAN

The early centuries AD witnessed the production of small bronze boxes, possibly used for jewellery, of which ten are known to date. These boxes, which are unique to Ireland, were furnished with lids ornamented in very sophisticated interpretations of the local Celtic La Tène style. The best known and most complete box in the series is that from Somerset, Co. Galway, which contained a gold ribbon torc and a small enamelled bronze ornament. The lid shown here is from a bog in Cornalaragh and features what is arguably the most sophisticated ornamentation of the whole series. The background was cut away to produce an openwork design consisting of a central disc at the centre of an open lattice pattern of lozenges.

D: 7.4cm, depth: 1.5cm   NMI REG. NO. ex-Shirley collection 33

27 Balline hoard CO. LIMERICK

This hoard of silver, containing ingots and scrap, was brought to Ireland from Britain about the fourth century AD, possibly by the Desi who raided southern Britain, a practice which was also to bring (the later St) Patrick to this island. The rough treatment of the silverware shows that it was the precious metal and not its shape or classical decoration that was prized by Celtic craftsmen.

NMI REG. NO. 1940.1a–g

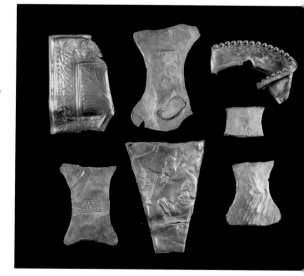

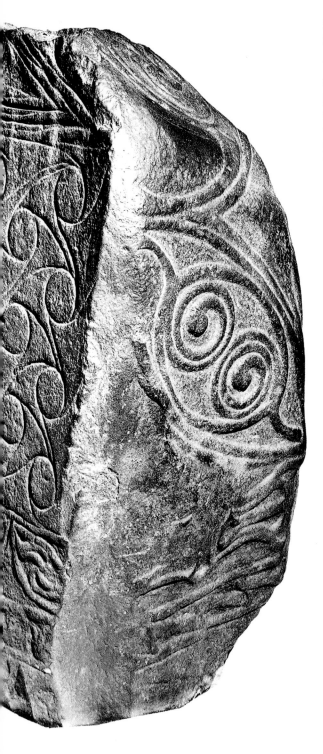

28 Mullaghmast stone
CO. KILDARE

This somewhat enigmatic artefact appears to be an anachronism in the pagan Celtic tradition of decorated symbolic standing stones, which date to the centuries around the birth of Christ, yet its ornament places it at the end of the developed native La Tène tradition, possibly about the sixth century. Sculpturally it is probably a link between the pagan and Christian eras, especially with the cross-inscribed pillars and decorated slabs of the latter. Its purpose is unknown; it may have been the commemorative monument of the transitional period when sculptors or their patrons were not sure of the iconographic needs of incoming Christianity, or didn't yet go along with it. The damaged nature of the stone and its discovery in a demolished medieval castle do not help to establish its purpose. The triskele on top, the pair of spirals with the clubbed terminal within the pointed oval at the side, as well as the highly geometrical arrangement of engaged 'peltae' or C-scrolls down the left side parallel the ornament on contemporary metalwork, such as that seen on the latchet brooch (see No. 29).

H: 1m, W: 37.5cm   NMI REG. NO. 1903.254

29 Enamelled bronze 'latchet' brooch

This cast bronze brooch consists of a disc attached to an S-shaped tail. There are traces of red enamel in the sunken field around the central triskele, as well as around the pair of tightly opposed spirals in the flattened-out expansion of the tail. The brooch is thought to belong to the fifth- to seventh-century period. It is an unusual type of garment fastener which may have been worn as part of a pair, supplemented by wires coiled around the tails. The triskele motif with bird-head terminals on the spirals, the thickly lobed spirals and the 'peltae' or C-scrolls outside the enclosing circle of the main motif are typical of the ultimate La Tène style motifs produced by native Irish metalworkers.

D: 5.7 × 5.9cm   NMI REG. NO. W492

30 Zoomorphic penannular brooch, Arthurstown CO. KILDARE

Such brooches are described as 'zoomorphic' because the flattened terminals of the rings are deliberately made to resemble animal foreheads, the snout parts being directed up the ring. The flattened areas allow for elaborate decoration, in this case a series of thin interlocking 'peltae' or C-scrolls in the ultimate La Tène tradition, with champlevé red enamel floated into the sunken area around the scrolls.

This brooch, from the sixth/seventh century, is one of the earliest types of Irish penannular (gapped ring) brooch, which was produced in many versions until the 'gap' went out of fashion in the eighth century.

D of ring: 8.55cm, L of pin: 16.8cm
NMI REG. NO. X1675

31 Ballinderry brooch CO. OFFALY

This enamelled bronze brooch, probably from the seventh century AD, was found during the excavation of Ballinderry crannog No. 2. It is one of the most impressive of our zoomorphic brooches; the animals' snouts are directed up the ring while the foreheads are flattened to take fields of ornament, in this case platelets of millefiori glass laid into red enamel. Such penannular brooches represent the last great flourish of the native metalworker's skill before the widespread incorporation of interlace into the repertoire and the advent of even more elaborate brooches like those from Tara (see No. 39) and Cavan (see No. 40), in which the gap between the terminals was bridged (a type termed 'pseudo-penannular'). The Ballinderry brooch was fastened by a long pin, the barrel-shaped head of which gripped the ring. The pair of bronze wire coils on the ring was probably intended to facilitate fastening by holding the pin in place on the garment.

W of ring: 8.6cm, L of pin: 18.3cm   NMI REG. NO. E6.422

32 St Patrick's bell CO. ARMAGH

This bronze-coated iron bell is traditionally thought to have been used by St Patrick himself and to have been buried in his tomb, from where it was later taken to Armagh and venerated for centuries. It is one of two types of Irish Early Christian bell (the other was of cast bronze) and was made in the sixth- to eighth-century period. A shrine was made for it later (see No. 55).

H: 19.3cm   NMI REG. NO. R4010

33 Crucifixion plaque

This openwork gilt bronze crucifixion plaque is one of the earliest representations of the Crucifixion in Ireland and is reputed to date to the eighth century. It is thought to be a book-cover decoration, although the possibility of its being associated with a large composite shrine, cross or altar has also been suggested. The decoration on the tunic, with interlocking 'peltae' or C-scrolls and tightly wound spirals, in what might be regarded as an ultimate La Tène expression in repoussé bronze, has been taken as evidence of an earlier date, possibly even the late seventh century. However, the perfection of many of the metalworker's techniques and the maturity of the figured scene suggest a later date.

L: 21.1cm   NMI REG. NO. R554

34 Donore door handle CO. MEATH

This animal-head handle with its escutcheon plate and frame are part of an early-eighth-century hoard, which also included another bronze ring-handle, a bronze-coated iron ring-handle and an engraved tinned-bronze plaque and frame. It is thought that the items in question were mounted on part of a church partition or tomb-shrine and concealed at a time of danger. It is possible that they came from one of the nearby churches, such as Kells or Dulane.

Comparison has been made between the decoration on the handle and that on the Lindisfarne Gospels and the Tara brooch (see No. 39), which date to about AD 700, and it has also been suggested that the handle is a local version of the lion-head door handles of ancient Rome, which had religious and ceremonial significance. The decoration itself, however, is purely Irish.

Ds of ring: 13.5cm; 10.1cm   NMI REG. NO. 1985.21b/d/e

35 Ardagh chalice CO. LIMERICK

This mid-eighth-century ministerial chalice is an exquisite example of the Irish Early Christian metalworker's craft and is probably the most famous object in the National Museum. The chalice is part of a hoard of objects found at Ardagh, Co. Limerick, in 1868. It consists of a silver bowl and conical foot which are separated by a gilt bronze stem. The names of the apostles (except Judas) are incised in a frieze around the bowl, below a girdle bearing inset gold wirework panels of animal, bird and plain geometric interlace. The handles and the escutcheons below them, as well as the side roundels, feature impressive gold filigree panels and glass studs with inset metal grilles. The underside of the foot bears a large round setting with a conical crystal at its centre. The out-turned flange of the foot bears panels of decorated bronze and knitted silver wire, between which are low translucent blue glass studs whose patterned silver foil mounts may be seen through the studs. The chalice was used for dispensing Eucharistic wine to the faithful.

H: 17.8cm, D of rim: 23.1cm   NMI REG. NO. 1874.99

36 Ardagh hoard CO. LIMERICK

The Ardagh hoard consists of the world-famous silver chalice, a bronze chalice, three brooches of so-called pseudo-penannular type and a 'thistle' brooch. Except for the latter, which is of early tenth-century date, all the items date to the eighth century. The hoard was found in 1868 at Reerasta ringfort near Ardagh. The objects were buried at a depth of one metre and were apparently partly protected by an upright stone. It is possible that the hoard was concealed for safekeeping during a period of (Viking?) raiding activity in the tenth century, when Limerick was the second most important Scandinavian settlement in Ireland. The magnificent silver chalice with its balanced design and perfect proportions of plain and decorated areas remains the finest surviving specimen of Irish Early Christian metalwork of the eighth-century Golden Age, despite similar claims in relation to the contemporary Derrynaflan paten (see No. 37).

Bronze chalice H: 11.8cm, max D of rim 13.8cm, depth of bowl: 6.7cm   Silver-gilt pseudo-penannular brooch D of ring: 13.1cm, max W of terminal: 7.58cm, L of pin: 22.55cm, D of ring: 9.2cm   Silver-gilt pseudo-penannular brooch L of pin 26.4cm, F of ring: 9.72cm, W of terminals 5.7cm   'Thistle' brooch L of pin 17.9cm, D of hoop: 7.65cm, average D of terminals: 1.56cm   Silver-gilt pseudo-penannular brooch D of ring: 13.1cm, max W of terminal: 7.58cm, L of pin: 33.55cm   NMI REG. NO. 1874.99-104

37 Derrynaflan hoard CO. TIPPERARY

The Derrynaflan hoard, which was found in 1980 on the monastic site at Derrynaflan, consists of a silver chalice, a silver paten and accompanying stand, a liturgical strainer or sieve, and a bronze basin which was placed over the other objects when they were buried. The objects date to the eighth and ninth centuries and were probably concealed about the same time as the Ardagh hoard (see No. 36). Derrynaflan is even more emphatically a hoard of liturgical vessels than Ardagh, which despite its two chalices has a higher number of secular items. The technical perfection of the twelve gilt copper-alloy settings (for inlaid enamels), which helped hold in place die-stamped gold foil panels (with trumpet-scroll and spiral motifs), is a remarkable feature of the paten. The twenty-four filigree panels are also noteworthy; by using combinations of gold wire and gold strips on edge, subjects including kneeling men, fanged beasts, snakes and eagles are brilliantly depicted. The paten was assembled according to a code of letters and symbols on the surfaces of the silver and on the detachable components.

Chalice max H: 19.cm, min H: 18.75cm, rim D: 20.7–21cm, bowl D: 16.7cm   Paten and stand max D 35.6–36.8cm, max H (incl. foot): 6.85cm, footring D: 3.5cm   Strainer/ladle L: 37.8cm, bowl D:11.5cm, bowl D:4.7cm, basin D: 44–46cm, H: 18–19cm   NMI REG. NO. 1980.4–8

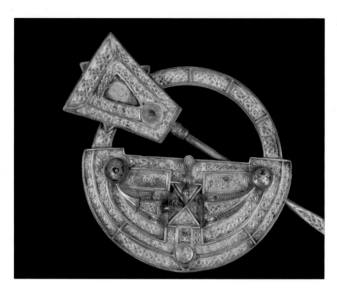

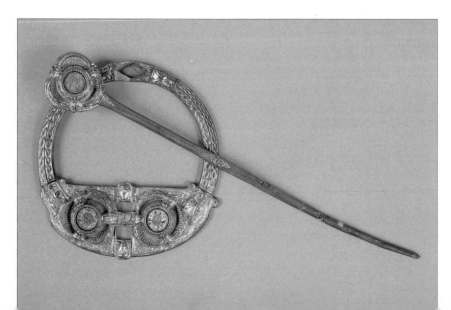

38 Ardagh silver-gilt brooch CO. LIMERICK

This very large and over-elaborate example of a pseudo-penannular brooch was part of the
hoard found at Reerasta ringfort, near Ardagh, in 1868, which contained the famous chalice (see
No. 35), a plain chalice, a second smaller and plainer pseudo-penannular brooch, as well as a
'thistle' brooch (see No. 36). Unlike the smaller pseudo-penannular brooch, the ring of the larger
specimen is completely closed, with the terminals making up a large D-shaped plate covered
with chisel-ornamented strips of plain interlace ranged around three birds in high relief (probably
modelled on a bone backing). The decoration on the pinhead echoes that on the plate. The
missing central triangular setting may originally have retained a matching raised-bird decoration.
Only one of the studs of the settings on the pinhead and plate survives; it is silver, with inlays of
glass.

D of ring: 13.1cm, L of pin: 33.55cm   NMI REG. NO. 1874.104

39 'Tara' brooch, Bettystown CO. MEATH

This early-eighth-century silver-gilt pseudo-penannular brooch is among the best known of all
the antiquities in the National Museum. It was found in 1850 on the beach at Bettystown, the
name 'Tara' being applied to enhance its value and to associate it with a findplace of appropriate
status. The beaded wire beast in the panel at the centre of the pinhead, the cast glass human
heads on the tags at the side hinge and the elegance of the pure Celtic design on the reverse are
particularly noteworthy.

   The rather Germanic front face with filigree animal interlace in the large left panel and in the
main panel of the pinhead, as well as the cast animal and bird heads that project from the outer
margins of the ring and pinhead, contrast with the reverse face (illustrated here) in which the two
large panels feature the most elaborate ultimate La Tène style spiralled triskeles.

D of ring: 8.7cm, L of pin: 32cm   NMI REG. NO. R4015

40 Silver-gilt brooch CO. CAVAN

This specimen is probably of ninth-century date, coming late in the series of Irish pseudo-
penannular brooches. The concentration of lavish decoration on the two terminals as well as on
the pinhead parallels the arrangement on the more impressive eighth-century series that
includes the Ardagh (see No. 38) and Tara (see No. 39) specimens. The roundels in the terminals
and pinhead bear simple circle and back-to-back C-scroll devices in beaded wire, with clusters
of gold granules at the centre. The roundels are accentuated by deep chisel decoration. This
ornament is often called the 'Queen's Brooch' because it is alleged to have been offered to
Queen Victoria.

L: 147cm   NMI REG. NO. W43

41 Banagher cross shaft
CO. OFFALY

This sandstone high cross shaft, apparently of ninth-century date, originally stood at Banagher. Both sides and most of one face bear panels of geometric interlace and interlinked C-shaped spirals. The other face features two scenes of life in Early Christian Ireland. Apart from the illuminated manuscripts, we have to rely on the sculptured panels of high crosses for representations of the Early Christian period in Ireland. The depiction of a stag caught in a deertrap on one panel of this shaft is of interest. The other panel tells us about horse type, horseriding, harness (or the lack of it), as well as clerical (?) garb. The long-tailed small pony on which the rider sat without spurs, stirrups or saddle, with the rider's legs forward, is confirmed from other sources, as are the flat-topped hairstyle and the crozier.

H: 146cm, max W: 39.5cm, T: 18cm
NMI REG. NO. 1929.1497

42 Carrowntemple slab CO. SLIGO

This is one of twelve carved slabs found in Carrowntemple in 1973, along with a slab roughout, inscribed fragment and cross(?) plinth. It is the only one that is carved on both sides. The front, not illustrated here, features a pair of triple-strand ribbons interwoven in a cross motif, with a fret pattern further down. The fragmentary remains of a church, possibly medieval, have also been discovered on the site. The graveyard is part of an enclosure that conforms to the pattern of the native monastic site of Early Christian Ireland.

It is not known what the figure is meant to represent. The head is disproportionately large, surrounded by a border and separate from the body, emphasising the primitiveness of a composition which, on the basis of the other side, could date from the eighth/ninth centuries. The other slabs in the series appear to have been meant to lie flat, while this specimen was intended to stand upright.

L: 121cm, W: 47cm
NMI REG. NO. 1986.3

43 Viking Age bossed and 'thistle' brooches and armrings

The Vikings seem to have found 'the cold gleam of silver' irresistible. While some of this precious metal may have been mined in Europe, especially after the mid-tenth century, most of the earlier silver came to Scandinavia as coins from trade with the Arab world. Silver flooded into Ireland as part of an international trade network, in which Dublin was especially important. Significant amounts of Irish Viking silver found its way to native chieftains, whose craftworkers converted it into an exquisite range of ornaments, among which were four main types: bossed penannular brooches (top pair and bottom right), bracelets (bottom left) and armlets, 'thistle' brooches (centre pair) and kite-shaped brooches (not illustrated). It is not certain whether the silver was handed over as tribute, for 'protection' or in the course of commercial exchange, or whether it was a combination of these.

44 Kite-shaped brooch CO. LIMERICK

The tenth century saw the production of many new silver ornaments, of which the kite-shaped brooch is the most distinctively Irish. 'Kite' brooches were worn on the shoulder, with the pin pointing upwards and the ring at the tip securing it to the cloth. Such large brooches may have been regarded as somewhat vulgar displays of wealth in the tenth century, when silver was increasingly used as a currency medium. The specimen featured here consists of a pendant attached by means of a hinged tag to a long pin. The pendant is lozenge-shaped, with animal heads at the angles. The heart-shaped opening at the centre recalls contemporary wooden ornaments, such as a harness-bow crest. Only half a dozen silver 'kites' are known, all from Ireland. Apart from the type illustrated here, smaller copper-alloy 'kites' have been found in excavations in Dublin. Large specimens with almond-shaped heads are also known, including one with sunken filigree panels not dissimilar to those depicted on the shale trial-piece from Christchurch Place (see No. 45). Related and possibly English-inspired star-shaped brooches of lead-alloy were also made in Viking Age Dublin.

L of pin: 51.3cm   NMI REG. NO. 1874.73

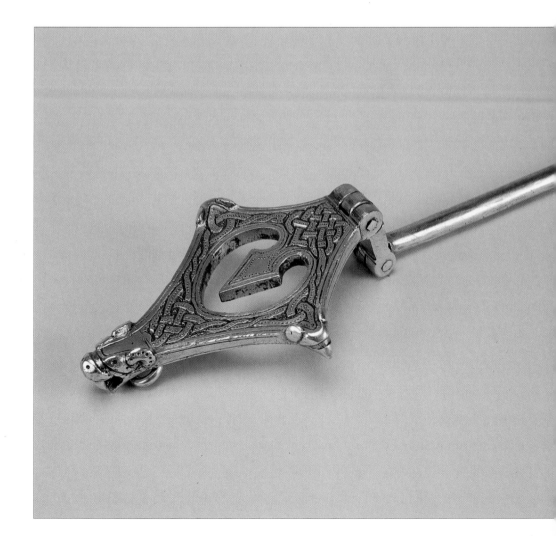

45 Bone trial- or motif-pieces Lagore CO. MEATH and Dooey CO. DONEGAL

Trial- or motif-pieces are usually small portable bone or stone pieces which bear carved or raised designs, ranging from the trial runs of apprentices and artist's sketches to the more deeply executed dies and models of metalworkers. This Irish tradition was later adopted by the Hiberno-Norse craftworkers of Dublin and other towns.

The eighth- to early ninth-century motif piece from Lagore crannog features panels with animals with curled jaws and spiral hip-joints; these parallel the finest metalwork of the eighth and early ninth centuries. The deeply carved Dooey piece (lower picture) is regarded by Uaininn Ó Meadhra and Raghnall Ó Floinn as the earliest Irish motif piece, possibly dating to the fifth or sixth centuries, that is, almost from the time of St. Patrick. It is a piece of antler and includes four closely grouped panels of three running spirals, shown here.

Lagore L: 22.2cm; Dooey L: 12cm   NMI REG. NOS. W29 and E33:385

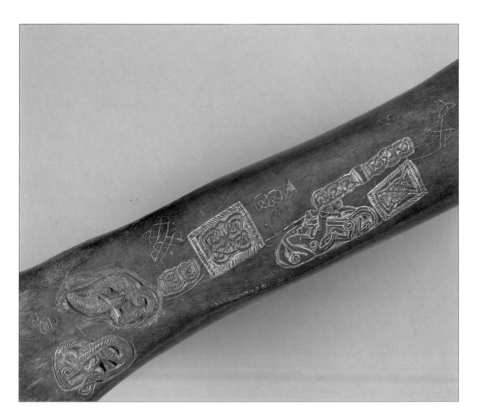

46 Selection of artefacts, Dublin excavations

This selection of objects from the Museum's Dublin excavations includes green and purple porphyry strips which are thought to have been brought to Dublin as souvenirs from Christian contexts in Rome. The function of the wooden mount with its carved openwork cockscomb terminals is not known. The ornamentation is an example of the Dublin expression of the mid-eleventh-century Viking art style known as 'ringerike'. The carved wooden figure, possibly a bottle stopper or game-piece, also attests to high-quality wood carving in Viking Dublin. The plaited gold ring and bracelet and the amber pendant are probably also of local manufacture and reflect the wealth of the town. The fact that amber would have had to be brought in from the Denmark/Baltic Sea area suggests that commercial links must have existed. The selection dates from the tenth and eleventh centuries.

47 Wooden boat, Winetavern St, Dublin

This carved wooden replica of a contemporary ocean-going Viking longboat is most likely to have been a toy. Viking ships were built in Dublin, as demonstrated by the tree-ring growth pattern in the keel of the warship found at Roskilde, Denmark and from the numerous ships' planks which were excavated on the Wood Quay/Fishamble Street site.

L: 36cm   NMI REG. NO. E81:432

48 Clonmacnoise crucifixion plaque CO. OFFALY

The single-piece plaque, which may have been part of a shrine or pyx, shows the framed figure of Christ (with outstretched arms and out-turned feet) flanked by the spoon-bearer and the spear-bearer, the crosses of the two thieves and, perched on Christ's arms, winged angels. The plaque is cast in bronze and on art-historical grounds may be dated to the eleventh century (particularly the half-palmette designs on the eight panels into which Christ's garment is divided). Although it has been suggested that plaques of this type may have been made in Clonmacnoise itself, it is worth noting that contemporary trial- or motif-pieces, especially from Hiberno-Norse Dublin (see No. 45), bear similar ornament, and it is possible that items such as this, as well as crozier-shrines, were made in Dublin to the order of bishops and abbots or their patrons.

L: 8.38cm, W: 7.26cm   NMI REG. NO. 1935.506

49 'Soiscél Molaise' shrine, Devenish CO. FERMANAGH

This box, believed to be the oldest of the eight surviving Irish book shrines, was made to enshrine the gospels of St Molaise of Devenish, Co. Fermanagh. The survival of an eighth- or ninth-century hinge on its side implies that it may be a remodelled version of an earlier reliquary. As it now stands, it is almost all of early-eleventh-century construction. The shrine was acquired from the O'Meehans, its hereditary keepers.

The front face (shown here) is laid out as a ringed cross with rectangular terminals, with panels of gold filigree and gilt silver framed by the silver grille of the cross device. The figures represented in the panels are the symbols of the four Evangelists, whose names appear in Latin on the margins. There is a request for a prayer for Cennfailad (the abbot of Devenish, 1001-25) who commissioned the shrine and for Giolla Baithin, the smith who made it, inscribed in Irish on one side of the shrine, while another side shows an interesting representation of an ecclesiastic in a tunic and cloak, holding a book and flail.

H: 14.75cm, W: 11.70cm, T: 8.45cm   NMI REG. NO. R4006

50 Shrine of the Stowe Missal, Lorrha CO. TIPPERARY

This shrine once contained a ninth-century Latin massbook that is now housed in the Royal Irish Academy, Dublin, which was thought to have been written either at the monasteries of Tallaght, Co. Dublin, or Lorrha, Co. Tipperary, near where it was discovered, sealed up in the walls of Lackeen Castle. It is called 'Stowe' because it was formerly stored at Stowe House, Buckinghamshire, England.

The shrine, which is made of wood and covered with metal plates, is mainly of the mid-eleventh century, but it was severely embellished in the fourteenth century when an entire face (shown here) was redesigned with the implantation of a rather vulgar silver-gilt cross jewelled with rock crystals, glass studs and an ivory bead (possibly modern). Plates of gilt silver show the Crucifixion and other scenes, and around the margins gilt silver plates inscribed in Irish ask for a prayer for Pilib (Ua Cennetig), King of Ormond 1371-81, his wife Aine Domhnall Ó Tolari, who repaired the shrine, and Giolla Ruadhan Ua Macain, the prior of the Augustinian priory of Lorrha.

L: 18.7cm, W: 15.8cm   NMI REG. NO. 1883:614a

51 Shrine of the Stowe Missal (detail), Lorrha CO. TIPPERARY

Apart from the mainly fourteenth-century face (opposite), the chief points of interest in this shrine are the mid-eleventh-century inscription on the other main face (dating to 1042–52) and the eleventh-century gilt bronze and openwork plaques, which are significant both for their representations of contemporary characters (mostly clerics and soldiers) and for their depiction of contemporary artefacts. On the side shown here there is a centrally placed plaque with a pair of clerics on either side of a seated figure playing a lyre, under an angel. The character on the left clutches a handbell with a pronounced clapper and wears shoes, in contrast to the barefooted figure on the right who holds a crozier. The clerics are wearing long tunics and ornate shoulder mantles similar to those on the Breac Maedhóg (see No. 53). On the opposite side of the shrine (not shown) a bearded figure is depicted holding a Viking-type sword between a pair of animals.

52 Clonmacnoise crozier
CO. OFFALY

Traditionally associated with the abbots of Clonmacnoise, the crozier consists of a crook and two tubular lengths of sheet bronze wrapped around a wooden staff, with three spacing biconical knops. Mainly of the eleventh century, with some fifteenth-century refurbishment, it is especially notable for the wonderfully bold snake-like animals in figure-of-eight arrangements, executed in inlaid silver and outlined with niello decoration on both faces of the bronze crook, and for the animals in the cast openwork ring under the topmost knop.

The crook was cast in one piece. There is an openwork crest comprising a procession of gripping dogs on top. The figure of a mitred bishop slaying a monster with his crozier, like the bearded head at the top of the drop, is late medieval.

The animal ornament on the sides of the crook is a version of the mid-eleventh-century international style known as 'ringerike', in which Hiberno-Norse Dublin had a distinctive school of woodcarving, now recognised as 'the Dublin style'. The discovery of similar designs, including the characteristic figure-of-eight type, among the Dublin trial- or motif-pieces (see No. 45) suggests that items such as this could have been made in Dublin.

L: 97.1cm   NMI REG. NO. R2988

53 Shrine of the Breac Maedhóg (detail), Drumlane CO. CAVAN

This house-shaped shrine, of which the O'Farrellys were the traditional keepers, dates to the eleventh/twelfth century AD. It is of particular importance due to the applied panels with well-observed, deeply cast figures, as well as interesting details of ecclesiastical and social historical interest. This section from the plaque on the side of the shrine shows a line of clerics whose tunics are clearly delineated. A late medieval leather satchel for this shrine is also on display at the National Museum.

L: 30.5cm, W: 12.7cm   NMI REG. NO. P1021:1022

54 Lismore crozier CO. WATERFORD

This crozier, which contains a wooden staff, was made about 1100 and was found in 1814 in a blocked-up doorway at Lismore Castle, together with a fifteenth-century manuscript. The name of the smith who made the crozier and the bishop of Lismore (1090–1113) who commissioned it are inscribed in a strip under the crook.

The crook was cast in one piece and is hollow, except for a small box-shaped reliquary inserted through a side in the drop. The border around the (now missing) front of the drop consists of panels of zoomorphic interlace that were originally covered in gold foil and separated by rectangular panels of blue and white millefiori glass in chequerboard arrangements. Distinctive blue glass beads with red and white millefiori insets form the main punctuation islands between the sunken panels that adorn the sides of the crook. The crest consists of three animals linked in openwork 'urnes' style interlace. Urnes is named after the decoration carved on the lintel and jambs of a church doorway at Urnes, Norway. Typically, the crozier also has slightly decorated upper and middle knops, as well as a lower knop which was cast in one piece with the ferrule.

L: 116cm   NMI REG. NO. L1949.1

55 Shrine of St Patrick's bell CO. ARMAGH

This shrine was made about the eleventh century as a container for the bell (see No. 32). Its side panels and crest are decorated in the so-called 'urnes' style in which large beasts are interlaced with thin ribbon-like snakes. An inscription on the margins of the back plate tells us that it was made by Condulig Ua hInmainen and his sons for Domhnall Ua Lochlainn (King of Ireland, 1094–1121). Domhnall Mac Amhalgadha was then bishop of Armagh, and Cathalan Ua Maelchallain was the 'keeper of the bell', a position his family was to retain until the end of the eighteenth century.

H: 26.7cm, base 15.5cm   NMI REG. NO. R4011

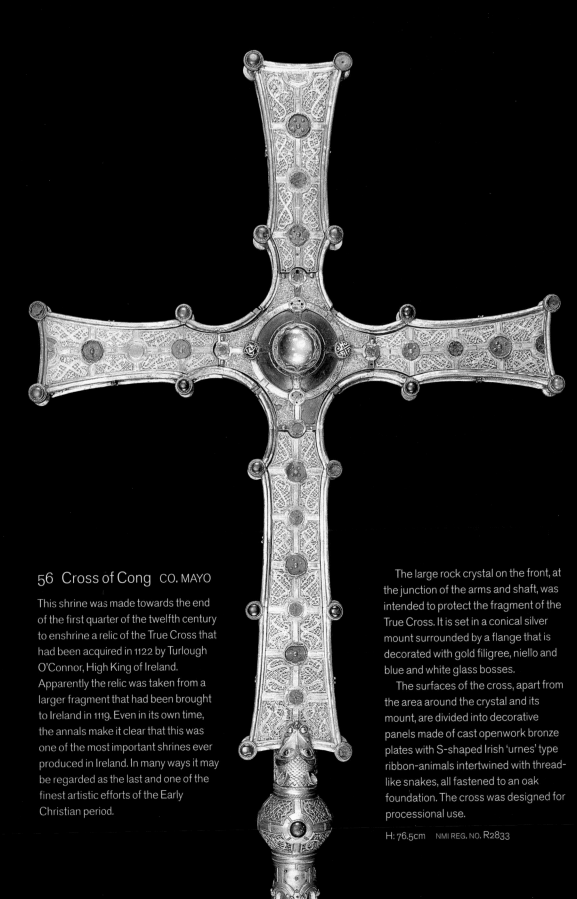

56 Cross of Cong CO. MAYO

This shrine was made towards the end of the first quarter of the twelfth century to enshrine a relic of the True Cross that had been acquired in 1122 by Turlough O'Connor, High King of Ireland. Apparently the relic was taken from a larger fragment that had been brought to Ireland in 1119. Even in its own time, the annals make it clear that this was one of the most important shrines ever produced in Ireland. In many ways it may be regarded as the last and one of the finest artistic efforts of the Early Christian period.

The large rock crystal on the front, at the junction of the arms and shaft, was intended to protect the fragment of the True Cross. It is set in a conical silver mount surrounded by a flange that is decorated with gold filigree, niello and blue and white glass bosses.

The surfaces of the cross, apart from the area around the crystal and its mount, are divided into decorative panels made of cast openwork bronze plates with S-shaped Irish 'urnes' type ribbon-animals intertwined with thread-like snakes, all fastened to an oak foundation. The cross was designed for processional use.

H: 76.5cm   NMI REG. NO. R2833

57 Shrine of the Domhnach Airgid, Clones CO. MONAGHAN

Originally of the late eighth or early ninth century, the main decorative panels are of the mid-fourteenth century with some fifteenth-century embellishment. Associated with the Maguire family, one of its most interesting panels (lower, left) shows a seated St Patrick presenting a book (the relic) to St MacCairthinn, patron saint of Clones.

L: 23cm, W:16.7cm, T:9.8cm   NMI REG. NO. 2834

58 Ballymacasey (Ballylongford) cross CO. KERRY

This late-fifteenth-century processional cross of gilt silver is one of the few examples of altar plate or church furniture from the late medieval period, when there was such a vigorous output of architecture and sculpture, as instanced by the numerous friaries that were established. It was found in 1871 during the ploughing of reclaimed bogland.

The cross bears a figure of Christ crucified and stands on a collar, knop and socket. It is also noteworthy for the openwork quatrefoil terminals with figures of the symbols of the Evangelists at the ends of the limbs, for the foliated outlines, and for the Gothic inscription in Latin on the arms and shaft, which tells us that Cornelius, son of John (and Eibhlin) O'Connor, 'head of his people', had it made by a William O'Connor in 1479. John had founded the nearby Franciscan friary at Lislaghtin, and this cross was given to the friary in his memory.

H: 67.2cm, W: 51.2cm, D of socket: 4.5cm   NMI REG. NO. 1889.4

59 Jugs and 'Piggybank', DUBLIN

Pottery appears not to have been produced in Ireland in the Hiberno-Norse phase, although pots were imported from Anglo-Saxon and Saxo-Norman England as well as from Normandy and northern France from the later eleventh century. The arrival of the Normans in the 1170s brought more pottery from south-west England and Bristol in particular. The broadening of trade contacts connected with wine imports also brought fine wares from France, especially from the Saintonge region around Bordeaux. The jugs on view here came from Bristol (right) and Saintonge (centre pair) as well as from Dublin (left): the piggybank was made in Dublin. All the vessels shown here date to the thirteenth century, the Bristol jug being the earliest. The Bristol and Dublin jugs and the piggybank were found at the museum's excavations at Wood Quay, and the French pair at nearby Winetavern Street.

60 Maori side-post or 'poupou', New Zealand

The National Museum's ethnographic collections came originally from Trinity College to which James Patten, a surgeon on Captain Cooke's second voyage, and Captain James King, on the third voyage, presented their eighteenth-century Maori collections. The focal point of the traditional Maori community was the *marai* or open space, where people gathered, and its associated meeting-house, where individuals assembled to discuss matters relating to the tribe as well as to sing, dance and play games. The meeting-house became the symbol of tribal power and wealth. The layout of the house also replicated the body of an ancestor. It was elaborately carved and extended up to thirty metres in length. The wall posts on the inside of the house were usually carved in the shape of a human figure, as can be seen in this example.

L: 109.1cm   NMI REG. NO. 1898.349

61 Benin bronze head

This African ceremonial bronze head is currently part of the Museum's ethnographic collections. The bronze head was used as the base for a tusk on an ancestral altar in the Oba's Palace in Nigeria's Benin kingdom. It was brought to Europe following the destruction and subsequent looting of the city of Benin by British troops in 1897.

H: 40cm   NMI REG. NO. 1898.190

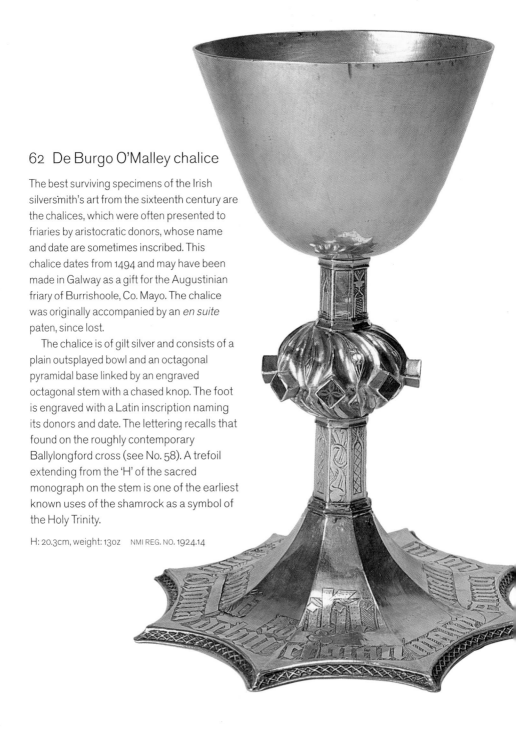

62 De Burgo O'Malley chalice

The best surviving specimens of the Irish silversmith's art from the sixteenth century are the chalices, which were often presented to friaries by aristocratic donors, whose name and date are sometimes inscribed. This chalice dates from 1494 and may have been made in Galway as a gift for the Augustinian friary of Burrishoole, Co. Mayo. The chalice was originally accompanied by an *en suite* paten, since lost.

The chalice is of gilt silver and consists of a plain outsplayed bowl and an octagonal pyramidal base linked by an engraved octagonal stem with a chased knop. The foot is engraved with a Latin inscription naming its donors and date. The lettering recalls that found on the roughly contemporary Ballylongford cross (see No. 58). A trefoil extending from the 'H' of the sacred monograph on the stem is one of the earliest known uses of the shamrock as a symbol of the Holy Trinity.

H: 20.3cm, weight: 13oz   NMI REG. NO. 1924.14

63 Silver candlestick

The Rococo style marked a departure from the solid forms and simple decorative motifs of the preceding Baroque era in its display of exuberant asymmetrical forms and decoration. Developed under Juste Aurele Messonier, Director of the Royal Factory in Paris, the style was disseminated through his published engravings. The engravings were counterfeited in London by John Rocque in 1737; they were most likely available in Dublin some time later. Rocque did in fact come to Ireland in 1754 to make his celebrated maps of Dublin city. Dublin, as the established economic, social and political centre of Ireland, possessed a well-established silver trade, making objects which mirrored prevailing foreign fashion and taste. Rococo arrived in Ireland in the 1740s, having already established itself in England by 1720.

   The elements of Rococo, as seen in this candlestick (which is one of an identical pair), include C-scrolls arranged asymmetrically, combined with vines, scrolls used to form a cartouche for armorial bearings, repoussé designs raised using a hammer, with the ornament forming an integral part of the shape. This candlestick was made by Robert Calderwood who worked in Castle Street from 1740 to 1755 and in Cork Hill from 1756 until he died ten years later.

H: 29cm   NMI REG. NO. 1952.10

64 Silver tea urn, Dublin

Demand for domestic silver increased greatly during the seventeenth century. The influx of French Huguenot silversmiths influenced design and manufacturing. During the eighteenth century the Anglo-Irish entertained lavishly, reflecting a hitherto unseen level of elegant living in Ireland. The tea urn was used to keep water hot at the table and was fitted with either a spirit lamp or charcoal burner underneath, or with a socket inside to hold a hot iron. The tea urn shown here was made by Robert Breading in Dublin in 1808. It stands on four reeded legs with pan feet on a base supported by four ball-rests and is fitted inside with a cylindrical holder for a hot iron. Its inscription tells us that it was presented by the Tipperary militia to John C. Douglas, the regimental surgeon.

H: 35.5cm   NMI REG. NO. 1976.1

65 Lord Chancellor's mace, Dublin

A symbol of authority and badge of office, the mace is carried before, or by, officials of various ranks. A crowned mace is ceremonial, symbolising the Royal power as delegated, in part, to a mayor or other officer of a corporation. This mace was made by William Townsend of Dublin somewhere between 1760 and 1770 and belonged to the Lord Chancellor of Ireland. It consists of a large canopy with four compartments decorated with shields and with Britannia seated.

L: 148cm   NMI REG. NO. 1925.21

66 Silver sauceboat, Dublin

Silver vessels have adorned Irish tables since at least the seventeenth century. Among those used to serve liquid foods were cream jugs, sauceboats, hot water jugs (for serving coffee, chocolate and hot milk as well as water), soup ladles, large soup bowls or tureens, sauce ladles (much smaller than soup ladles, for serving sauce from sauceboats), argyles or gravy pots, and herb or saffron pots, which are like small teapots.

About 1735, sauceboats with a single pouring lip and a handle opposite became popular. Some sauceboats were set on a collet or stemmed foot, while others were fitted with three or four legs. This sauceboat was made by Thomas Walker about 1747. It is a fine example of Irish Rococo silverware and features typical maritime motifs such as applied fish, sea-shells and, on the handle, the sea-god Triton.

H: 27.94cm, W: 46oz   NMI REG. NO. 1955.31

67 Silver tea set, Dublin

The mid-nineteenth-century growth of interest in Ireland's ancient past, coupled with the discovery of significant relics such as the Ardagh chalice (see No. 35), led to the popularity of a revived Celtic art style which was applied to objects in the decades before and about the turn of the century. In silver, ancient art objects (especially brooches) were copied and contemporary articles like this tea set were decorated with neo-Celtic motifs, such as patterns of interlacement and stylised animal forms.

The set here consists of a cream jug, sugar bowl and teapot made in 1870 and a hot water jug made in 1874 by John Smith.

Teapot H: 14cm, W: 29cm; coffeepot H: 22cm, W: 22.5cm; bowl H: 9.4cm, W: 19.6cm; jug H: 10.5cm, W: 11.6cm
NMI REG. NO. 1979.18-21

68 Vodrey vase

Frederick Vodrey was born in Staffordshire and moved to Dublin in 1861 with his widowed mother. Although not a potter himself, Vodrey, through his talent as a designer and businessman, established a successful pottery factory in Moore Street. The collection of Vodrey pottery presented to the National Museum in 1886 by Vodrey himself represents the variety of stylistic derivations typical of decorative arts in the late nineteenth century — Moorish, Celtic and Japanese aesthetics. Vodrey's designs thus reflected his awareness of contemporary trends in their transition from the purely classical form and ornament to those of Celtic revival and Japanese design. This vase is an example of wheel-and-lathe-turned glazed earthenware and in its austere simplicity is indicative of the growing interest at the time in Japanese taste.

H: 30cm, D: 15cm   NMI REG. NO. 1886.105

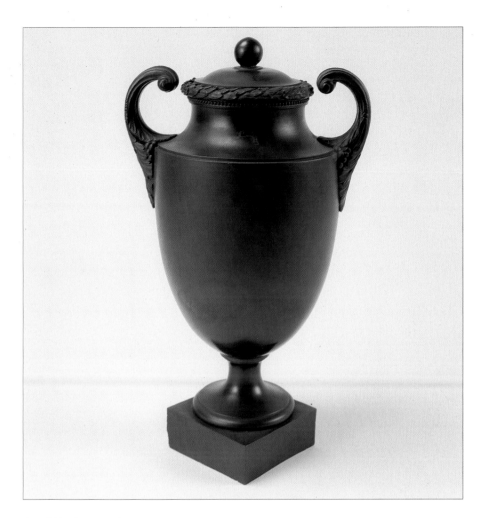

69 Wedgwood vase

In the late seventeenth century and especially during the eighteenth century artists, scholars, architects and educated gentlemen travelled more and more widely visiting and reporting on ancient monuments in Greece and Egypt. The more widespread dissemination of information and the procurement of actual objects led to the emergence of neo-classicism. The neo-classical style was based on the simple geometric forms of ancient Greek and Roman architecture and ornament. Josiah Wedgwood, in partnership with Bentley, opened a pottery factory in 1769 producing ceramics such as this vase. These were well suited to the neo-classical style of architecture, furnishing and interior decoration. The vase is an early example of basalt ware, a hard fine-grained black stoneware resembling the hard black igneous rock often used by the Egyptians for sculpture. The vase makes appropriate stylistic references to ancient classical design in its material, form, proportion and ornament.

H: 10.75cm, D: 6cm   NMI REG. NO. 1891.87

70 Sèvres vase

Sèvres, the French national porcelain factory, was renowned in the luxury trade, becoming a fashion leader from about 1760. Originally founded in 1738 at the Chateau de Vincennes, the factory was removed to a purpose-built premises at Sèvres in 1756. In 1759 the Sèvres factory was taken over by King Louis XVI, who became its chief client and salesman, bestowing Sèvres porcelain services on many royal and foreign dignitaries. This vase and cover is decorated with a *pate sur pate* classical female figure. Although used in eighteenth-century China, *pate sur pate* was rediscovered at Sèvres soon after 1851. A process of creating decoration in relief, *pate sur pate* is achieved by applying layers of white slip, which, allowed to dry between applications, is carved using metal instruments.

H: 38cm, D: 14cm   NMI REG. NO. 1882.3950

71 Delamain dish, Dublin

Delftware has a soft earthenware or baked-clay body covered with thin enamel and was first developed in Antwerp and the Low Countries in the sixteenth century. The first delftware factory in Ireland was established in Belfast in 1698. Perturbed by the scale of imports, the Dublin Society (later the Royal Dublin Society) offered a premium to anyone who could establish a delftware facility in Dublin. The challenge was taken up by Captain Henry Delamain in 1752, when he began producing dinner services, spirit barrels, wall-fountains, small fruit baskets and apothecaries' jars. Some designs were copies of Chinese or Japanese motifs, others were views of country residences, more had landscapes, coats-of-arms or crests. The delftware charger shown here was made at Henry Delamain's pottery, Dublin, about 1752. It was hand-painted in blue, probably by Peter Shee, landscape artist and clerk at the pottery.

D: 36cm   NMI REG. NO. 1924.122

72 Belleek porcelain figure of 'Hibernia' CO. FERMANAGH

Belleek, Co. Fermanagh, is synonymous with the production of the first hard-paste porcelain in Ireland. Their porcelain was acclaimed during the nineteenth century for its light weight, iridescent glaze and rich ivory colour. 'Hibernia awakening from her slumber' is considered to be among the earliest figures designed for and made at the Belleek pottery. Designed by William Boyton Kirk, Dublin, it was made about 1865 and was first exhibited at the Dublin Exhibition in the same year. 'Hibernia' with her harp and cross – symbols of Ireland – unveils a classical urn representing the Belleek pottery. She stands on a flagstone of the waterfall from which Belleek derives its name.

H: 44cm   NMI REG. NO. 1970.76

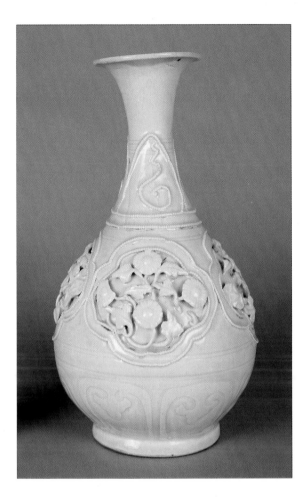

73 Fonthill vase, China

This vase has the unique artistic and historic significance of being the only extant example of porcelain to have left China in the early fourteenth century whose history and movements can be traced virtually unbroken to the present day. It was made in China about the thirteenth century, during the Yuam dynasty, probably at Jingdezhen in the Jiangxi province. This became the centre of the Chinese ceramics industry under the Mongols, who brought skilled craftworkers from all parts of Asia, especially Persia. In the later fourteenth century the vase was owned by Louis the Great of Hungary, who had a set of silver-gilt accessories made for it. By the early eighteenth century it had become the property of the Dauphine of France, and at the end of that century it was bought by William Beckford of Fonthill Abbey in Wiltshire, England. Later it was bought by the Duke of Hamilton and stored near Glasgow until 1882 when it was bought for the National Museum of Ireland.

H: 28cm   NMI REG. NO. 1882.3941

74 Commemorative glass, Cork or Waterford

This early-nineteenth-century goblet was produced in urn form. The beautifully executed commemorative engraving is from the end of the nineteenth century and features the 'Corporation of Ardfert', Co Kerry. It is presently on loan to the Kerry County Museum, Tralee, along with the Hayes chalice and O'Connell memorabilia (including the duelling pistols) subject to annual renewal.

H: 25.4, D at lip: 14cm
NMI REG. NO. 213.1972

75 Penrose decanter, Waterford

George and William Penrose, members of a Quaker family which settled in Ireland during the seventeenth century, opened a glass factory in Waterford in 1783. Although the factory only lasted in Penrose ownership until 1799, the glass produced not only supplied the home market, but was exported as far away as the West Indies. The glass made at the Penrose factory was in the fashionable English style. A popular style of decanter made by Penrose was barrel-shaped, with three triple neck rings, a large flat lip and moulded flutes carried onto the base. This decanter, made about 1790, is undecorated and exhibits the Penrose style in its barrel shape, neck rings, flat lip and basal moulded flutes.

H: 20cm, D: 9cm
NMI REG. NO. 1943.49

76 Tieze goblets

During the nineteenth century there was a marked increase in demand for engraved glass. The glassworks of Thomas Pugh (1819-1903) and his elder brother John (1805-79) enjoyed a high reputation for the production of engraved glass. The company is generally referred to as that of Richard and Thomas Pugh (Richard was Thomas's son). They were in charge when these goblets were made.

Glass engravers from Bohemia such as Franz Tieze worked in Dublin during the second half of the nineteenth century. On coming to Dublin in 1865, Tieze found work with the Pugh glassworks. The goblets here were probably made by Pugh in the 1880s and engraved by Tieze. Fashion and taste in Ireland at the time dictated the use of nationalist iconography which embodied the design idiom of the Celtic revival and included the round tower, wolfhound, harp and shamrock together with phrases such as 'Erin go Bragh'. A sketchbook belonging to Tieze, which is now in the Victoria & Albert Museum, London, clearly illustrates that he was using such motifs in his designs for engraved glass. The tendrils of shamrocks seen on these goblets were a characteristic trademark of Tieze's engraved designs.

H: 15.8cm   NMI REG. NO. 1974.44/45

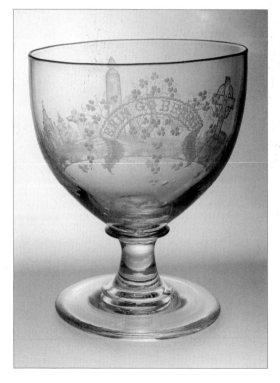

77 Glass vase, Stourbridge, England

The removal of the excise tax on glass in 1845 enabled many British glass manufacturers to experiment and attempt new techniques of production, which was reflected in the demand for ornamental glass in the 1850s. Cameo glass consists of a piece of glass with an overlaid second and sometimes third layer of different coloured glass. The outer layer is partially cut away to reveal a pattern or figurative scene in colour against the background. By the 1880s, glassworks such as that started by Thomas Webb of Stourbridge in 1837 were producing ornamental glass of which cameo was a part. As a reaction to the mechanisation of glass production throughout the nineteenth century, there was a marked revival of techniques for making and decorating expensive ornamental glass for a wealthy and appreciative market. Cameo glass used decoration and required a high degree of technical skill in its production. Unfortunately, by the 1890s the continued influx of cheap imports and increased industrial mechanisation meant that cameo glass of this quality became too costly and unaffordable.

H: 13cm, D: 12cm   NMI REG. NO. 1885.348

78 Loetz vases, Klostermühle, Czech Republic

At the end of the nineteenth century the impetus for glassmaking shifted to the United States and continental Europe with developments in iridescent glass. Iridescence is the rainbow effect of different colours caught at varying angles of illumination and is produced naturally by the effect of acids on glass that has been buried in the soil for centuries, as in the case of some Roman glass. It was being produced commercially in Bohemia as early as 1867, with the use of metal oxides, and was popularised in the 1890s by the great innovator and pre-eminent American designer Louis Comfort Tiffany. At the same time, glassworks such as that of Loetz in southern Bohemia, where these vases were made, were experimenting in iridescent glass, displaying their successful results at exhibitions, including that at Vienna in 1898. Over the next decade the glassworks produced decorative effects using iridescent spots, ribbons and threads of gold, silver, blue, purple and amber. The irregular twisted bodies and rims of the vases, together with the use of fluid lines and elaborately twisted tendrils, embody the Art Nouveau style for which this type of glass was well suited.

H: 17cm, D: 9cm   NMI REG. NO. 1900.496

79 Killarney furniture CO. KERRY

Killarney, with its surrounding picturesque mountains and lakes, developed a tourist industry from at least the early nineteenth century. A market for the production and sale of souvenirs inevitably resulted. In the 1820s souvenirs consisted of small wooden items carved out of local bog oak and yew. They reached their peak of popularity during the 1850s, but were in decline by the 1880s. During the 1840s the production of furniture became a means of augmenting the seasonal nature of the trade in smaller goods. The high quality and what was considered sophisticated design of the Killarney furniture led to its display at national and international exhibitions at London (1851), Cork (1852), Dublin (1853), London (1862), Dublin (1865). Typical inlays consist of pictorial views of local landmarks and wildlife, as well as floral trails and sprays and, of course, the Irish harp.

H: 115cm   NMI REG. NO. 1981.5

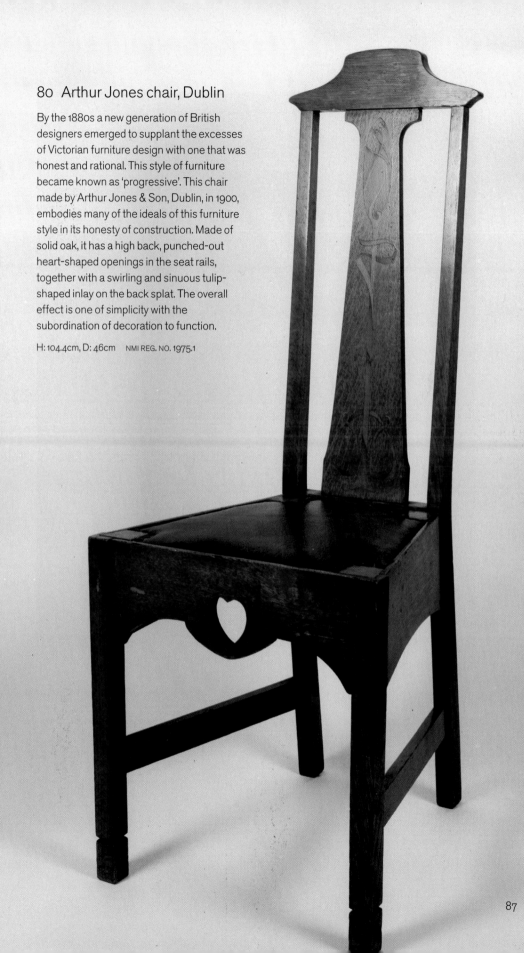

80 Arthur Jones chair, Dublin

By the 1880s a new generation of British designers emerged to supplant the excesses of Victorian furniture design with one that was honest and rational. This style of furniture became known as 'progressive'. This chair made by Arthur Jones & Son, Dublin, in 1900, embodies many of the ideals of this furniture style in its honesty of construction. Made of solid oak, it has a high back, punched-out heart-shaped openings in the seat rails, together with a swirling and sinuous tulip-shaped inlay on the back splat. The overall effect is one of simplicity with the subordination of decoration to function.

H: 104.4cm, D: 46cm   NMI REG. NO. 1975.1

81 Egan harp, Dublin

From the earliest times the harp has been associated with Ireland. During the early nineteenth century, John Egan, Dawson Street, Dublin, was considered to be the most important and innovative harp maker. Reflecting this reputation, he was appointed as harp maker to the Crown between 1800 and 1840. Although Egan's harps retained much the same shape as the ancient variety, they were far lighter in construction and followed fashionable taste in their decoration. The large pedal harp here was made in 1820 and reflects the contemporary classical fashion with its corinthian column, caryatid figures and anthemion in gilt relief. The sound box is white pine with gold Greek and floral scrolls.

H: 180cm   NMI REG. NO. 1907.190

82 Harpsichord, Venice

The harpsichord is a stringed keyboard instrument differentiated from the piano in that its strings are plucked rather than struck. The earliest known reference to the existence of the harpsichord dates from 1397, while its earliest representation can be found on a fifteenth-century German altarpiece. The instrument remained in use until the eighteenth century and fell into complete disuse by 1810. A large number of surviving harpsichords date from sixteenth-century Venice, which appears to have been the most important centre for the design and production of harpsichords. This Venetian harpsichord dates from 1560 and is heavily decorated with marquetry veneer, featuring various hunting scenes. It was acquired by the National Museum in 1887.

H: 215cm, L: 202cm, W: 79cm   NMI REG. NO. 1887.240

83 Astrolabe, Czech Republic

Astronomy originated in the ancient world and is probably the oldest of the sciences. One of the tools of astronomy, the astrolabe, believed to have been invented in Egypt, was known in Europe by the tenth century. It was used to measure angles, to determine time and altitude and to calculate the position of the celestial bodies. This piece was made for Dr Francisci de Padoaris, physician to the Austrian emperor, Rudolf II, and was designed by Erasmus Habermel of Prague in the early seventeenth century. It is part of the Museum's collection of scientific instruments, which includes instruments used in surveying, optics, astronomy, measurement and chemistry.

D. 17cm   NMI REG. NO. 1899.499

84 Plate sundial, Dublin

This is an inclining plate sundial made by Seward of Dublin. The development of the sundial was stimulated by the advent of clocks and watches, because of the need to monitor their accuracy. The inclining plate sundial could be used in more than one latitude by adjusting the dial against an attached degree scale. The instrument illustrated here dates from the mid-eighteenth century. Dublin enjoyed a considerable reputation for the production of quality scientific instruments, with names like Grubb, Mason, Spear, Spencer and Yeats.

H (extended): 10.4cm   NMI REG. NO. 1910.578

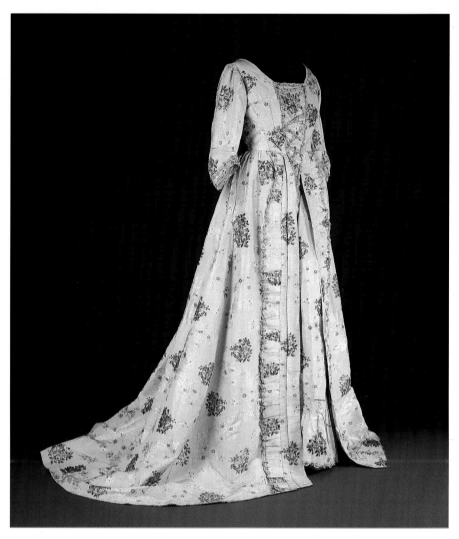

85 Robe and petticoat, Dublin

Throughout the eighteenth century, women's dress consisted of a gown or overdress comprising a bodice and open skirt joined together to reveal a petticoat underneath. The petticoat was not considered to be an undergarment but rather an integral part of the dress. Short sleeves and low necklines were also a common feature of fashion. Although remodelled for the centenary celebration in 1898, this cream silk brocade dress still displays some fashion features from the preceding century – it was made about 1775 – with its overgown and ruffle to the hem, petticoat with deep ruffle, low neckline, short sleeves and choice of rich material. The fabric is reputed to have been made in the Dublin Liberties for Mrs Peter Tone, mother of the hero of the 1798 rebellion, Wolfe Tone. It was altered to fit a descendant, who wore it at the centenary celebrations of the rebellion.

Overdress L: 158cm; underskirt L: 98cm   NMI REG. NO. 1946.97

86 Lace flounce, Limerick

The most widespread of the Irish craft industries during the nineteenth century was lacemaking.
The lacemaking industry in Limerick was started by Charles Walker in 1829 on a purely
commercial basis. Although popular with Queen Victoria during the 1840s and 1850s, the design
and workmanship of Limerick lace had deteriorated to such a degree that the industry declined
by the 1870s. Limerick lace was revived, however, in the 1880s with the arrival of Mrs Florence
Vere O'Brien who set up a lacemaking school and worked to improve the standards of design
and materials. This flounce is made of tambour lace, which originated in the East and was not
known in England until 1820. Tambour lace is created by stretching net over a tambourine-
shaped frame. The cotton thread is pulled through the mesh by a crochet-like needle, thus
producing the design.

L: 74cm, W: 41cm   NMI REG. NO. 1898.197

87 Cameo pendant, London

Archaeological discoveries made an important impact on eighteenth-century artists, designers and craftspeople, who were able to see and explore, for the first time since the Renaissance, the art of the classical past. The neo-classical style, which was popularised by such discoveries, emerged during the early nineteenth century, as did the Etruscan style. Typical of the Etruscan style was the use of scenes in relief against a lighter or darker background as in this cameo. The cameo was a carved gem much used in the ancient world. This example was carved by Benedetto Pistrucci, an acclaimed Roman cameo portraitist. (On coming to England he joined the staff of the Royal Mint where he designed the new gold coinage.) The gold setting in which the cameo is placed was made by Augosto Castellani whose father, Fortunato, had been a jeweller in Rome.

L: 4.7cm, W: 3.4cm   NMI REG. NO. 1888.221

88 Giuliano gold pendant and chain, London

The pendant is in the form of Acheolous, the river god, and is based on an Etruscan prototype in the Louvre Museum. Made about 1860, it is part of a small collection of gold jewellery by Carlo Giuliano that was presented to the National Museum of Ireland by his sons in 1900. Giuliano, who died in 1895, was one of a number of master craftworkers who pioneered the revival of interest in the designs and techniques of Etruscan and classical jewellery during the nineteenth century. This occurred at the same time as Irish craftworkers were taking a fresh look at their early jewellery and making reproductions of Irish archaeological jewellery. This pendant shows Giuliano's mastery of the ancient techniques of gold soldering, gold wire drawing and granulation. Giuliano had been a student of Fortunato Castellani, who is credited with the revival of ancient goldworking techniques through his study of Etruscan jewellery. His son, Augusto, made the gold setting for the cameo pendant (see No. 87).

Pendant L: 4cm; chain L 42cm   NMI REG. NO. 3/4.1900

89 Swords, Dublin

A hand-held cutting or thrusting weapon, the sword probably evolved from primitive implements such as the axe. The basic design of the sword – a long broad blade with a simple form of cross guard hilt – remained the same until the sixteenth century. By the eighteenth century the sword was being standardised by governments for military purposes, but during the nineteenth century was replaced by the use of firearms and artillery on the battlefield. The sword on the left is from the Revenue Police, a force set up in Ireland in the 1820s, whose task was to suppress illegal distilling. The centre sword is an army officer's of 1803-22 with blued blade and gilt engraving. The third sword, on the right, is of a militia officer of about 1800.

Revenue Police sword L: 98cm   NMI REG. NO. 1913.1133

90 Head armour, Japan

The Diamyo were the upper echelon of the feudal lord system who, together with the Shogun and the Samurai, controlled Japan. The Diamyo warriors (1185–8) were considered to be patrons and practitioners of the arts, blending their warrior traditions (bu) with civilian arts (bun). This head armour is made from iron, leather and lacquered panels.

L: 30cm   NMI REG. NO. 1993.2d

91 Buddha image, China

This is a standing image with the hands in the *mudra* gesture and the face exuding a gentle friendliness. The statue was made during the Konbaung dynasty (1752–1885), using a dry lacquer inlaid with coloured glass. It has the essential characteristics of Sakyamuni Buddha: a large bump on the top of a head of curly hair, long pierced earlobes, monk's robes, bare feet and unusually long toes. The buddha holds a small medicinal fruit between the thumb and forefinger, having received such a fruit from the god Indra after his enlightenment.

NMI REG. NO. L. 221 (2a)

92 Pottery, Peru

The eathernware vessels made in Peru were among the finest produced in South America and are notable examples of pre-Columbian art. Although potters were producing ware as early as about 1200 BC, it was not until about 800 BC that distinctive ware with stirrup-shaped spouts emerged. This vessel is modelled in the shape of a seated man; his hands are on his knees and his head is surmounted by a winged bird.

H: 23cm, D: 18cm   NMI REG. NO. 1884.478

93 Sinn Féin flag CO. CAVAN

This 1917 flag of the Bailieboro, Co. Cavan, branch of the nationalist Sinn Féin party features Éamon de Valera, the senior surviving Volunteer commandant from the Easter Rising of 1916, after whom the branch was named. De Valera was imprisoned in a number of English jails before being released in June 1917. He went on to become one of the major figures in the subsequent War of Independence (1919–21) and survived to be successively President of the Executive Council of the Free State, Taoiseach and President of Ireland. He was also president of the League of Nations. The Museum has an extensive collection of memorabilia associated with figures such as Éamon de Valera, Michael Collins, Richard Mulcahy, Seán Treacy and Liam Lynch.

NMI REG. NO. EW1216

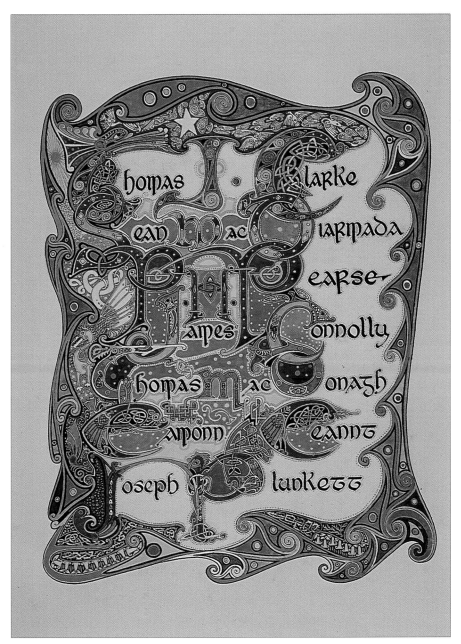

94 Leabhar na hAiséirighe, Dublin

Leabhar na hAiséirighe (Book of the Resurrection) by Art O'Murnaghan consists of twenty-six illuminated pages, of which the 'Signatories Page' is shown here. The book was commissioned in 1921 and was completed over a period of thirty years. It was intended as a memorial to those who had died in the fight for independence. The debt of its inspiration to Ireland's early Christian illuminated manuscripts is obvious. O'Murnaghan's work represents the best of Celtic revival style, of which Brian O'Higgins's Christmas card series was the most popular expression.

NMI REG. NO. EW78L

95 Cashman photograph, Dublin

The nonchalance of this bowler-hatted cyclist as he is searched by a British soldier shows that everyday life had to go on even during the War of Independence (1919–21). This photograph with its interesting social, military and technical detail (not least the bicycle!) is part of the Museum's Cashman Collection. Joseph Cashman (1881–1969) was an important photo journalist who worked for the *Cork Examiner* and *Freeman's Journal* (1911). He worked freelance from 1923 to 1929, when he was asked by Éamon de Valera to join the *Irish Press*.

NMI REG. NO. EW83 (Purch)

96 Domestic bread iron, Carrickacroman CO. CAVAN

Bread irons or oatcake toasters were used to bake the oaten-bread cakes that were eaten throughout the northern part of Ireland well into the present century. They were made of wrought iron and often show exceptionally fine workmanship. The specimen featured here was made about 1810 by a blacksmith called Martin Dowd who lived and worked in Clifferna, Co. Cavan. Unlike griddles, which were held in place by pot-hooks over an open fire, bread irons were placed in front of the fire. This one has a loop at the back to hold the stick that would have propped it up.

H: 47cm, W: 49cm   NMI REG. NO. F1960.77

97 Cailleach or harvest knot, Ulster

Celebrations at the end of harvest included the making of a harvest knot or cailleach from the last sheaf. The cailleach was then ceremoniously presented to the woman of the house. Common throughout Europe in the nineteenth century, it was thought that the last sheaf contained the spirit of the supernatural powers that inhabited vegetation. This spirit was thought to influence people's lives. This belief changed at the beginning of the twentieth century when the cailleach was considered a simple expression of delight at the completion of the major work of the year.

L: 30 cm   NMI REG. NO. 1945.7

98 Butterprint, Glencolumbkille CO. DONEGAL

Acquired for Folklife in 1936 from Glencolumbkille, Co Donegal, this butterprint was presented by a Mrs O'Donnell.

D: 9.8cm   NMI REG NO. 9.12.1936

99 Hair hurling balls

Hair hurling balls have come to light in bogs in counties Cork, Kerry and Limerick, and one was found in Sligo. The balls have been found at considerable depths in bogs, indicating that they could be as much as one thousand years old. Among the many historic references to the hurling balls are their association with the game itself, their creation for May Day hurling contests by newly-married women, their use by children as toys and their use as love tokens during the courtship period.

NMI REG. NO. 1975.153

100 Penal crosses, Ballintober CO. MAYO AND CO. TYRONE

Created as a souvenir of the pilgrimage to Lough Derg, Co. Donegal, the penal cross was a representation of Christ's crucifixion and passion. Many of the symbols used by the craftsmen were common in the early years of Christianity. These symbols first appeared in Ireland on family tombstones in the late Middle Ages. The survival of the symbols in religious folk art is testimony to the strength of belief and tradition through centuries of political and religious upheaval. The earliest known penal cross dates from 1702 and they were still being made in the mid-nineteenth century. Carved from wood, mostly yew, the design is generally stylised and geometric. Both crosses here show Christ, symbols such as a cock in or above a pot and the letters IHS or INRI. The cross found in Mayo is dated 1748 and portrays the thieves crucified alongside Christ.

Ballintober L: 17.9cm, W: 7cm, D: 6cm   NMI REG. NO. 1932.101   Tyrone L: 20.8cm, W:5. 3cm, D: 1cm
NMI REG. NO. 1949.11

101 Weaver's stamp

One of a pair of brass weaver's stamps which had wooden handles from Dungiven, Co Derry. One stamp has a harp at its centre, surmounted by a crown, while around the edge are the words 'The NY Montgomery Tully-Derry'. The second stamp bears three leaves of shamrock and at the top a harp with the word 'Derry' above it. Around the perimeter are the words 'William White, Limavady'.

H: 4.5cm; W: 5.5cm   NMI REG. NO. F1931:187, 188

102 Costume

The next group of entries, on costume, are photographs from the museum's archive, showing rural Irish clothing. These photographs are shown rather than photographs of items of clothing in the museum's collection, as they show the clothing in context, as worn by the people.

Throughout the nineteenth century there was a certain distinctiveness in the clothes of the women of rural Ireland. The fabrics were mainly homespun and uninfluenced by the fashion of the day. Women wore a woollen overskirt usually in red, black or dark blue, a flannel outer skirt, a simple blouse or bodice known as a *polici* or *corpán* worn either inside or outside the skirt and, most characteristically, a shoulder shawl made from wool and known as a wrapper or hug-me-tight.

103 Aran Island basketmaker

A basketmaker making a 'sciob' on the Aran Islands, Co. Galway, in the early years of this century. He is wearing traditional clothes including a *léine gorm* or blue shirt and *bheist* or short-sleeved jacket.

104 Men's clothing

This photograph taken on the Aran Islands about 1910 shows the uniformity of dress. Each of the men is wearing wide loose trousers of frieze held in place by a *crios* or belt. Their feet are protected by *troigthin* or knitted ribbed socks that reached the knee. The men on the extremes are wearing *bascota* or waistcoats made of white flannel. The knitted jumpers with their distinctive rope patterns later developed into the 'Aran' style still popular today.

105 & 106 Women's clothing

The woman in Photo 105 is dressed in a skirt made of drugget, a material with a woollen weft and a linen warp, and a *seál mór* or large shawl worn over her muslin cap. These caps were traditionally worn by married women for most of the nineteenth century. The woman on the right in Photo 106 is wearing contemporary clothing of 1910 made from imported fabric, while the woman on the left is wearing a more traditional costume displaying to great effect the wrapper or hug-me-tight. Their hairstyles indicate that they are single women.

107 Coracle, Slane CO. MEATH

This hide-covered currach from the river Boyne at Slane Castle demesne, Co Meath was acquired by the museum in 1928 for Irish Antiquities and subsequently passed on to Folklife. The currach was built around an ellipse, using thirty-two rods to form a basketry framework, the stout gunwale being formed by weaving strong withies around the rods. The frame was covered with tanned hide and immersed in water. Twines were used to attach the covering as well as the plank seat.

L: 208cm, W: 120cm, H: 66cm   NMI REG. NO. 1928.764

108 Man and donkey

This photograph shows a man from the Aran Islands collecting seaweed with his donkey. His *orléine ghlas* or blue flannel shirt is essentially a tunic with set-in sleeves and a narrow neckband. He is also wearing a *bheist* or waistcoat with white flannel on the front and blue frieze on the back. His trousers are also of blue frieze. On his feet he is wearing pampooties made by cutting salted hide into a shoe shape, leaving holes from toe to heel. These holes were then threaded with leather or fishing cord and tied across the instep.

109 Tollboard, Ballitore CO. KILDARE (overleaf)

The board sets out the tolls and custom of the fairs and markets of Ballitore, Timolin, Co Kildare. The board itself probably dates from the first half of the nineteenth century, though the tolls look high for that time. Sixpence in old money was a considerable amount for a breeches-maker to pay for the rent of his standing on a fair day, as indeed it also was for a cart-load of plants or earthenware or even woodturned bowls and plates. The practice of paying tolls goes back to murage tolls of the Middle Ages and beyond and was well known at turnpike gates from the mid-eighteenth to the mid-nineteenth century.

L: 77cm, W: 43.5cm, H: 1.2cm   NMI REG. NO. F1967.43

Tolls & custom of The fairs & Markets of Ballitore Claimed by Wm. LEADBEATER.

Black Cattle Per Head	4
Calves Pigs Sheep & Lambs Each	1½
Covered standings Each	8
Open Standings Each	6
For Each Standings of Timber Rakes Poles Shovel Handles & The Like	4
For Each Standings of Baskets Or Brooms	4
For Each New Fack Or Shovel	1½
For Each Car Of Plants Or Earthenware	6
For Each Car of Wooden Ware	6
Breeches Makers Standings Each	6
Brogue Makers Do Do	6
Butcers Per Car	6
For A cask Or Part of a Cask of herrings	6
For Each Hawker Or Pedlar	3
Bacon Salt Meat or buter Per Standing	4
For each Load of Ribberies	6
For Each Tent or Standing for Selling Porter ale or spirits	1 4
For Standing of Fruit Each	6
For Each Standing of Onions	6
For Each Sack Or Bag of Corn	1
For Each Sack Or Bag of Potatoes	1
For Each Bag of Meal Weighing Six Stone Or Upwards	1
For Each Lot of Fowl	1
Hatters Standings Each	6
For a car or cart of Pigs	6

110 Natural History Museum

The Natural History Museum was founded in 1792 and it moved from Leinster House to the present building in 1857. Described as one of the world's finest and fullest collections in the old cabinet style, this marvellous museum can still inspire wonder and amazement in young and old alike. There are extensive exhibitions of animals from all over the world. Geological specimens are also on display.

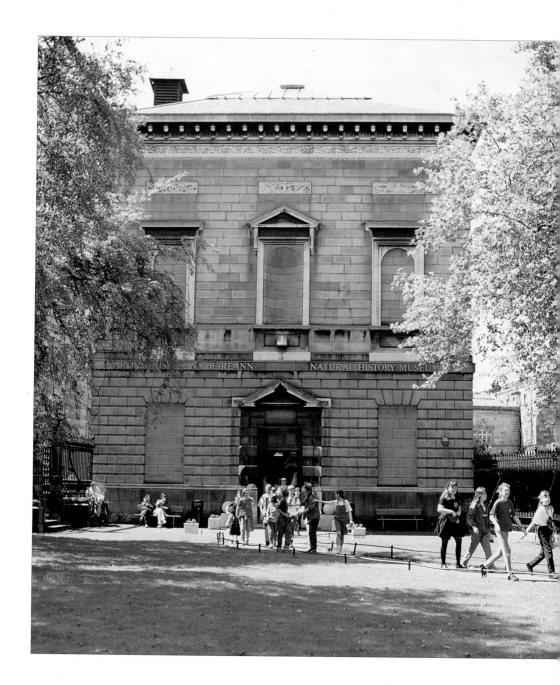

111 Blue peacock, India and south-east Asia

The blue peacock (*Pavo cristalus*) is a native of the forests and jungles of India and south-east Asia, but has been bred in captivity for about two thousand years. The male, shown here, displays his magnificent ornamented tail to the peahen by raising it up like a fan over his head.

2.m2 x 1.8m   NMI REG. NO. 306:1901

112 Fossil fish, Italy

This fish is from the same family as the scadepoch, that is, about fifty million years old. The fossil was collected by Rev George Graydon who presented it to the museum of the Royal Irish Academy on 1 March 1794, when he lectured on the nature of such fossils and their mode of formation. His friend, Hugh Hamilton, tried to reproduce the process of fossilisation and the work carried out by these two men was published by the RIA in their *Transactions* for that year.

17cm x 15cm   NMI REG. NO. F20639

113 Madagascan rayed tortoise

Tortoises belong to an ancient group of reptiles which were in existence at the time of the dinosaurs. The Madagascan rayed tortoise (*Testudo radiata*) is now confined to the far south of the island of Madagascar. This region is almost waterless, but has a plentiful supply of prickly pear trees, which provide the animals with food and shelter.

27cm × 15cm   NMI REG. NO. 23:1900

114 Long-horn beetle

A member of a large family of insects, the long-horn beetle varies greatly in size and appearance, but nearly all have unusually long antennae. Their wood-boring larvae can take several years to complete their development, during which time they can cause extensive damage to trees. The long legs of this Harlequin beetle (*Acrocinus longimenus*) from South America make it the largest beetle in the world.

6cm × 2cm (front legs 10cm)   NMI REG. NO. 1:1884

115 African butterfly

The dominant family of butterflies is the Nymphalidae, a diverse group comprising about five thousand species. Common Irish examples include the peacock and small tortoise-shell. The front legs of both sexes are degenerate and useless for walking. The species illustrated here is *Euphaedra francina*, which is widely distributed in the tropics of Africa.

6cm × 5cm   NMI REG. NO. 100:1900

116 Helmet shell

Helmet shells (*Cassis madagascan gensis*) live in sandy areas in the tropics and in temperate zones and prey on sea urchins. There are about sixty species, all of which are characterised by large body whorls and short spires. They are at home in the Bermuda/Caribbean and south-east United States areas. The species shown here is the black helmet. Shell enamel cutting developed during the fifteenth century. The different-coloured layers of shells make them ideal for cutting.

17cm × 12cm   No NMI REG. NO.

117 Nepalese tiger

The tiger (*Poanthera tigris*) is the largest of the cats. It has a wide distribution around the globe, including India, China and Siberia. It is mainly nocturnal, hunting mostly medium to large mammals. The National Museum's specimen is from Nepal and was presented by King George V of England in 1913.

1.6m × 1m   NMI REG. NO. 167:1913

Index